# churchmoney

"I love this book! Fr. Michael White and Tom Corcoran offer a powerful reminder that it is not what God wants *from* us but what God wants *for* us by connecting money to building our relationship with God, to our parish community, and to those we seek to bring into a personal and ongoing encounter with Christ."

**Bill Baird**
Former CFO for the Archdiocese of Baltimore

"Michael White and Tom Corcoran invite us to rethink Catholic giving by sharing crucial lessons from the personal experience of moving their parish's fundraising approach from one of obligatory tithing to true, inspired stewardship. They demonstrate the impact of utilizing best practices in increasing the offertory, extraordinary gifts, and planned gifts. An insightful book for both pastors and lay leaders to use in growing a thriving parish that transforms lives and builds the body of Christ."

**Josephine Everly**
Chief Development Officer
Leadership Roundtable on Church Management

"The genius of *ChurchMoney* is in the authenticity and generosity of Fr. Michael White and Tom Corcoran in sharing their real experiences and learning. They provide a trustworthy compass to help pastors and parish teams focus on what is most important in the funding of our parishes."

**Fr. Thom Mahoney**
Pastor of New Roads Catholic Community
Belmont, Massachusetts

"This book is such a blessing. As a pastor seeking to change culture, sow mission, and build vision, I found *ChurchMoney* a tremendous help bringing together various elements of parish finances: culture, education of the community, cultivation of donors, hints for fundraising, along with the authors' personal insights. Scriptural references, spiritual and pragmatic guidelines, and practical steps guided me to a new level of comfort and confidence in understanding and approaching money as a tool to help us in the making of disciples."

**Msgr. Robert J. Jaskot**
Pastor of the Pastorate of Saint Francis–Saint Mary–Holy Family
Middletown, Maryland

**Michael White and Tom Corcoran**

LESSONS FROM A CATHOLIC PARISH

# churchmoney

Rebuilding

the Way

We Fund

Our Mission

AVE MARIA PRESS AVE Notre Dame, Indiana

---

Founded in 1865, Ave Maria Press is a ministry of the United States Province of Holy Cross.

www.avemariapress.com

Paperback: ISBN-13 978-1-59471-912-7

E-book: ISBN-13 978-1-59471-913-4

Cover and text design by Andy Wagoner.

Printed and bound in the United States of America.

*Library of Congress Cataloging-in-Publication Data is available.*

# CONTENTS

# INTRODUCTION

It is important to lay out a comprehensive view of stewardship—a vision of a sharing, generous, accountable way of life rooted in Christian discipleship—which people can take to heart and apply to the circumstances of their lives. Concentrating on one specific obligation of stewardship, even one as important as church support, could make it harder—even impossible—for people to grasp the vision. It could imply that when the bishops get serious about stewardship, what they really mean is simply giving money.

—United States Conference of Catholic Bishops,
*Stewardship: A Disciple's Response*

Stewardship is a spiritual principle established by God when he placed the first human beings in a garden "to cultivate and care for it" (Gn 2:15). Subsequently, mankind has been invited to cooperate *and* collaborate in the work of creation and redemption. A comprehensive view of stewardship includes time, talent, and treasure—really the whole of our lives.

However, what follows is *not* intended to be such a comprehensive treatment of the subject. Instead, we are taking a long, hard look at just one aspect of the stewardship that our faith calls us to undertake. Because it is our contention that *this aspect* is too often overshadowed and overlooked—or conversely, misunderstood and misrepresented—in parish life. So, just so you know, when we get serious about stewardship, what we really mean is simply giving money.

This is a book about money in the heart of the Church—the *parish*. It's a book about *funding* our parishes, an important and increasingly critical issue determining the health and, in fact, the very life of churches everywhere. Apart from mere survival, through and beyond the current crisis, parishes will need robust funding to effectively undertake the work of the New Evangelization.

You should know when it comes to money and giving, we're certainly no Rockefellers. Neither of us has even taken a basic business class or economics course. We've made plenty of mistakes both in our personal finances and in the financial management of our parish. Our overall attitude toward money didn't help either: for a long time, we thought the whole idea of paying any attention to money was beneath us. As parish leaders, we had better things to do. And, if the full truth be told, we were uncomfortable with the topic; our discomfort was born of an ignorance of God's word and our own lack of giving.

However, as we have studied healthy, growing churches and their successful leaders, we've learned that financial stability and, indeed, strength are fundamental elements of a church's health and growth. Sure, they have compelling visions, God-honoring missions, and highly motivated staff cultures, none of which have anything to do with money. But they also have incredible facilities in amazing locations; huge, well-paid staffs; and state-of-the-art technology, all of which *does* take money. Lots of it.

Consider the largest, fastest-growing churches in the country: Elevation Church in North Carolina, Life.Church in Oklahoma, New Spring in South Carolina, North Point in Georgia, and Saddleback in California. They have taught their parishioners how to give and, in the process, have funded the unparalleled growth of their churches. It should not be forgotten that many of their parishioners are former Catholics. It turns out, Catholics *can* grow as givers.

Struggling to pay the bills because there's little financial margin is no fun. Not having enough money for staff salaries is stifling. It's heartbreaking to lay off people for lack of funds. Constantly begging, nagging, and even manipulating parishioners to give is annoying and never successful in the long term. Besides, it is self-defeating and demoralizing when their failure to respond leads to anger and frustration.

On the other hand, it's energizing and exciting to watch the offertory collection increase and the budget grow as parishioners match their commitment to the mission of your parish with their financial support.

Here are our credentials. While we do not live in a growing part of Baltimore County, during the last fifteen years our budget has tripled. In the same period, we have run three capital campaigns for new facilities, raising unprecedented amounts of money for a parish of our size and demographic. Our second campaign doubled the amount raised in the first. The third earned five times the second, and ten times the first. We sped past our goals, leaving the projections of our paid fundraising consultants in the dust.

Over the past ten years, our staff has quadrupled. Honoring a commitment made long ago, we've raised, and continue to raise, staff salaries. We want to provide living wages, excellent benefits, great health-care and retirement plans, professional development, and continuing education—all possible because of increased giving.

Expanded mission outreach has been another fruit of our congregation's giving. One project set a goal to raise money for a new high school facility for our mission partners in Nigeria. And then, we were thrilled to watch parishioners provide more than double the necessary funds. Our missionary efforts and giving have strengthened our partners in Haiti, Kenya, and our own city of Baltimore.

We're writing for pastors, pastoral associates, financial managers and accountants, development officers, financial and parish council members, donors and potential donors, and everyone interested in the financial health of their parish.

This book is intended to encourage you to reconsider current funding efforts and inspire you to embrace new behaviors and fresh approaches. We believe, properly implemented and consistently followed, the lessons that follow will dramatically change the finances of your parish. As your parish grows in its *financial* health—believe it or not—it will also grow in *spiritual* health.

And that, of course, is the most important growth of all.

# Part I
# MONEY AND OUR PARISH

# 1

# WHEN IT CAME TO MONEY, WE WERE A MESS

Jehoiada the priest then took a chest, bored a hole in its lid, and set it beside the altar, on the right as one entered the house of the LORD. The priests who kept the doors would put into it all the silver that was brought to the house of the LORD.

—2 KINGS 12:10

**Father Michael:** My first parish council meeting at Church of the Nativity proved to be unforgettable. And not in a good way. It quickly escalated from merely dysfunctional to deeply divisive. The tone was heated and the rhetoric harsh. The debate, I later learned, was a reprise of a long-standing conflict played out annually between rivaling factions.

On the right (the far right), the Ladies' Club (aka, the Altar Guild) in alliance with the Men's Club (aka, their husbands, the ushers) were fiercely defending the privileges and perks accorded their principle fundraiser. This project involved the insistent, extended, wholly annoying sale of "Entertainment Books" (fat, ugly, little volumes filled with worthless discount coupons for local restaurants nobody ever ate at and attractions few people wanted to frequent). The sale tediously stretched from Labor Day to the Fourth Sunday of Advent.

On the left stood the Youth Group (aka, the middle-aged youth minister and three middle school moms) aggressively advancing the rather intrusive claim of the group's Christmas wreath fundraiser. Given the seasonal nature of the product, their window of opportunity for sales was obviously limited. It spanned roughly Halloween through Thanksgiving, requiring an aggressive sales strategy.

At issue were the placement of bulletin ads and bulletin board posters, priority in pulpit announcements, and, most bitterly, the exclusivity of a coveted lobby sales table, a privilege enjoyed as a birthright by the Ladies' Club and only sometimes extended to the youth.

As the discussion unfolded, or rather unraveled, it became clear that, while the Youth Group had plenty of passion, they were no match for the Ladies' Club, who easily outgunned them with greater firepower. Eventually, the moms retreated, storming out with the denunciation that "this parish doesn't care about our kids!"

Here's the thing: neither fundraiser was raising funds for the mission of Christ's Church. The ladies were funding their monthly "meetings." These gatherings included lectures from local merchants on topics ranging from yoga to flower arranging, followed by dessert, coffee, and canasta. The youth minister was simply looking for money to underwrite the winter ski trip. Loving God, loving others, and making disciples were not considerations.

That evening was merely a primer to the problems we would encounter when it came to money and our parish:

- It was actually fussy and even complicated to commit to support us financially. In order to receive giving envelopes, you had to make a special trip to the parish office during weekday office hours (it couldn't be done on the weekend or online). However, the only person on staff who knew how to fill out the needed form kept irregular hours, so more than one trip might be necessary. Furthermore, the envelope company we used was notorious for failing to actually enroll new givers. So subsequent office visits might be necessary—for those motivated few who persevered in the process.

- About those envelopes: they were ugly and cheap. And the design seemed to *encourage* modest giving. Givers could check off a box on the face of the envelope corresponding to their gift: $2, $5, $8, or $10 were the options. Was it possible, one was left to wonder, to make a gift of *more* than ten dollars?

- There was a second collection almost every week with an accompanying giving envelope, usually even uglier than our own. These collections supported a bewildering variety of obscure causes: "Catholic Communications," "Summer Maintenance," and "Black and Indian Missions," just to name a few. Yielding only a small percentage of our regular, or first collection, most of these offerings were, tellingly, received in cash. And, not coincidentally, there was never any explanation about what these collections supported or where the money went.

- That is, except for December's second collection, for retired religious. On this particular occasion, a frail, elderly nun would painstakingly trudge up to the pulpit. Between breaths, she chronicled the sacrifice the retired sisters had made over numerous generations, all the while receiving only subsistence compensation, with no provision for their retirement. Often looking as though she was expending her last full measure of strength to make this appeal, it was always the largest collection of the year.

- We would come to recognize, in the culture of the parish, an unhealthy interest in how "you" (the parish staff) were spending "our" (the parishioners') money. There was a preternatural alertness to evidence of any expenses whatsoever. Even among many of our best givers, this "us versus them" attitude toward money prevailed. They adopted the convenient perspective that the parish staff already had all the money we needed. Any suggestion that we needed *more money* was evidence to them that we were spending beyond our means.

- All that said, we'll admit that we were not at all strategic about our spending. We didn't budget with our mission in mind, nor did we always honor our budget. And that did nothing to encourage confidence in our fiscal leadership.

- In fact, there really was no budget or budget process. Beyond the fixed costs of running the parish, how we spent money was an ongoing, open negotiation. If a staff member wanted money for anything, they had to go hat in hand to the accountant and plead for funding. After requests were reliably denied, appeals would often be made to the pastor. His decisions were final—unless he *approved* the expense, in which case the accountant would appeal. Usually the last one to have the pastor's ear got their way.

- Worse still, we were guilty of stupid spending: liturgical vestments and décor we couldn't afford, musical programming our parishioners didn't really want, and elaborate seasonal decorations and displays that were wholly unnecessary.

- And meanwhile we were foolishly ignoring other financial considerations that should have been of concern.

**Father Michael:** Staff salaries, for instance, were a scandal. During my first week, I interviewed the staff I had inherited, each of whom demanded some kind of raise. Although their timing was unhelpful, and their sense of entitlement was disturbing, I had to agree that their level of compensation was appalling.

- Our financial "advisors," the finance council, were a collection of deliberately divisive pals of the former pastor, who had no financial background or insight. They were dysfunctional, counterproductive, and pugilistic. Their agenda was to defend the spending of the previous administration and denounce any new fiscal patterns or priorities we were proposing. As a result, council meetings were fractious and demoralizing.

- Financial irregularities abounded. The parish accountant was a ninety-year-old volunteer, who kept the Dickensian-style ledger books of our accounting "system" in his basement. The money counters were the same old boys club who served as the financial council, responsible for financial oversight. Since they were also the ushers, that meant they collected the money, counted it, and took it to the bank. Nobody thought there was a problem with that.

- The culture of the money counters was toxic: a number of them didn't even go to Mass; money counting *was* their church attendance. On Sunday mornings, they would drink coffee, eat donuts, count the money as it came in, and gossip (mostly about us).

- And we were running an annual deficit with no savings of any kind. Financially, we lived week to week. If the Ravens had a one o'clock football game, or the county schools had a three-day weekend, or the weather was bad (or the weather was especially nice), attendance was down. And that automatically meant the collection would be down too. In turn, there would be unpaid bills that week. We always had lots of unpaid bills.

- When it came to financial reporting, there was no accountability. Once a year, we offered a financial "report" read at Mass in place of the homily. This fifteen-minute presentation was given by members of the financial gang. The report offered little information. It was, more or less, an invitation from bullies daring anyone to question the management of parish finances. The message was clear: *If you don't like the way we do things, you can leave.* Most people could not have cared less.

- There were no development efforts of any kind. At all. *Ever.* Period. Our parish simply didn't lift a finger in the direction of giving or the cultivation of givers because the pastor did not want to be beholden to anyone. His basic attitude was the same one we initially adopted ourselves.

- The narrative that had been spun by the previous administration made it very difficult to suggest that our finances were anything other than great. In the words of my predecessor, they were in apple-pie order.

In fact, when it came to money at Nativity, we were a mess. And the mess we inherited we proceeded to turn into an even bigger mess.

That's not inconsistent with what's going on nationally and elsewhere around the world. The financial issues facing the Church are so myriad and far-reaching, just beginning to name the problems is a challenge. But maybe the best place to begin is at the beginning, with this simple, basic fact: Catholic giving is not good.

Catholics give at the lowest level of giving among all Christians. All of them. We're in last place—by a lot. Catholics give at about half the rate of Protestants and a quarter (or less) the rate of Evangelicals. That's a problem, and it's a long-standing problem—in fact, a historic one. And it's getting worse:

- It's getting worse when it comes to deferred maintenance that is rendering the Church's vast collection of facilities unusable and, increasingly, unsalvageable.

- It's getting worse through unfunded retirement costs, unpaid insurance premiums, and neglected diocesan taxes and assessments.

- It's getting worse in the widening disparity between the need to attract more lay staff and the prevailing inability to pay them.

- It's getting worse in our increasingly underfunded youth programs and music ministries, leaving our parishes uncompetitive in the highly competitive marketplace that now characterizes churchworld.

Meanwhile, parishes in much of the country are combining or clustering, oftentimes wedding financial instability with more financial instability. Elsewhere, communities are financially limping along toward their inevitable demise.

In his excellent study on the subject, *Why Catholics Don't Give*, Charles Zech walks us through some of the substantial data available to support these assertions. One fact alone should sound the alarm: our current pool of givers is aging quickly, and new generations are not giving at the level of previous generations, if at all. That study is now thirteen years old and the situation seems to have only grown worse. We could very well be on the precipice of a cataclysmic loss of income.

So why don't Catholics give? Well, it's actually easier to identify things that are *not* the causes of this situation. First of all, it has nothing to do with income. While the immigrant Church of a century ago was certainly impoverished, today there is virtually no difference in household income levels between Catholics and Protestants.

Another oft-cited reason for low giving is that Catholic school tuition colors and clouds the equation. Certainly, parishioners who are paying tuition and parishes who are inevitably hosting school fundraisers find themselves in a complex scenario. And in that complexity, the lines between parish and school support are blurred at best. Doubtless, there are some who use their tuition payments as an excuse for failing to support the parish financially. But in fact, the data shows that Catholic school families usually give to their church at a *higher* rate than others in the parish.

It's not about parish size or demographics, and it is not a regional or ethnic dilemma. Giving can be a problem found everywhere, in all kinds of parishes.

Certainly, giving has been negatively impacted by the abuse scandal in the Church as well as the subsequent bankruptcies and payoffs. The economic consequences of the current crisis will most certainly be significant, though its full impact, as of this writing, has yet to be understood. However, the giving problem long predated these developments, and it does not seem to have escalated everywhere in tandem with fresh revelations, at least in the experience of most parishes.

It is often said that Catholics vote with their money. So, it has been argued that the lack of giving is a symptom of dissatisfaction with programs and services at the parish level, or policies and procedures at the universal level. That seems to be a reasonable argument to make, except that languid giving characterizes both the pre–Vatican II and the post-conciliar Church. And it is easy to identify parishes across the ideological, theological, and liturgical spectrum that are suffering from this problem.

Raising funds for a church is different than raising money for any other kind of charity. We didn't know that when we came to our parish. Nor did we realize that current giving in most parishes is not good. But rather than blame anybody, we propose a new way forward. You see, we believe the main problem when it comes to Catholic giving is a *cultural one*. As we discussed in our first book, *Rebuilt*, culture is the potent brew of knowledge, belief, and behavior, which everyone in an organization uniquely shares. And it can be the most powerful force of all. It affects everything: enthusiasm and morale, productivity and creativity, effectiveness and success. And money.

The reason so many parishes are facing financial problems is not because people will not give or cannot be inspired to give. It can't be blamed on the economy, and it's not a product of theological or ecclesiological disputes. We believe it's a *cultural problem* based on a misunderstanding of how the Lord taught us to fund his Church.

Elsewhere, Zech offered this insight: "The money crisis facing the Catholic Church is more than a money problem. It's a symptom of a larger problem: the decline of community and the confusion of purpose.

The way to raise more money for the Church is to become better at being the Church."

That is exactly what this book is about.

# 2

# CHRIST IS KING, BUT CASH IS CRUCIAL

## *5 FACTS WE'VE DISCOVERED*

*George*: I know one way you can help me. You don't happen to have eight thousand bucks on you?
*Clarence*: Oh no, we don't use money in heaven.
*George*: Oh yeah, that's right. I keep forgetting. Well, it comes in pretty handy down here, Bub.

—*It's a Wonderful Life*

**Father Michael:** A number of years ago, I had the unexpected idea of moving off campus for Christmas Eve. Not just offering another venue, we would instead be closing our church building completely and hosting Christmas at a facility that could accommodate the holiday crowds. Why not stop the ridiculous multiplication of Masses, gather everyone together for a real parish celebration, and provide space for visitors? It would illustrate a dramatic change in our church culture: doing church differently by getting out into the community and being accessible to them at exactly the time they want to visit us. We could make

Christmas Eve absolutely not at all about us and positively all about the people who were not in the pews. I loved the idea.

**Tom:** I thought it was crazy. And I was fairly certain that my reaction would be the typical one (just for the record, it was). That the facility, at the Maryland State Fairgrounds, was named the "Cow Palace" did not help our public relations campaign. Far and away one of our most unhappy parishioners was also one of our biggest givers. We'll call him "Jim" (since that was his name).

**Father Michael:** Word had reached me indirectly that Jim was more or less furious with our plan. So, reluctantly, I contacted him. I'm sorry I did. Given an opening, he blasted me with the full wrath of his fury. Beginning with a flat-out declaration that he and his family would be boycotting the event, he worked his way up to a crescendo, threatening to permanently withhold his annual contribution (which he eventually did). And since his yearly offering was almost equivalent to what it was going to cost us to host Christmas Eve, his threat essentially doubled the cost of the project. It was a very scary experience. We moved ahead anyway.

The amazing end to this story is that two days before Christmas, an unexpected donor showed up and wrote a check that covered the entire cost of the event, plus the equivalent of Jim's annual contribution.

Having money simplifies our lives and work. As my father is fond of saying, "Rich or poor, it's nice to have money."

A few years ago, our forty-year-old air-conditioning chiller gave out. We had hoped to squeeze a few more years out of it since we were already in the middle of a building project. But one weekend it finally decided to quit. For sure we had a problem, but that's precisely the point—we had *one* problem, not *two*. As a result of great leadership and good advice from our financial council, we could rely on a previously established emergency fund to pay for this unscheduled but inevitable expense. So, instead of having a chiller problem *and* a money problem, we only had to solve the chiller problem, which, with the necessary money in hand, was no problem at all.

Here are five facts we've discovered about money. They may not be news to you, but they were revelations to us.

# Fact 1: Money Is a Tool

Money is a tool, and a useful one, that was developed by groups of people to shape economies and build markets. It is sometimes labeled as the root of all evil, but it can also be a font of charity. Good or bad, it holds tremendous potential to influence society and change culture.

Admittedly, money can be an uncomfortable topic. And when it comes to money and the Church, well, that topic is even *more* uncomfortable. And that goes for churchpeople and the unchurched alike.

Talking about money in the Church evokes a long history of sin and corruption. A story is told of Thomas Aquinas being shown the renowned treasures of a great cathedral. Referencing Acts 3, where St. Peter said to a paralytic beggar, "I have neither silver nor gold, but what I do have I give you . . . [rise and] walk," the treasury official boasted, "No longer must the Church say, 'Silver and gold we have not.'" Aquinas retorted, "No, but neither do we have the power to say, 'Rise and walk.'"

The Church has often succumbed to the lure of money and wealth instead of relying on the power of God. History provides many examples of churchpeople making moral compromises and falling into malfeasance because of the pursuit or possession of money. After the conversion of the Roman emperor, Constantine, in AD 325, Church finances started getting complicated. What had been clear (albeit hostile) boundaries between Church and state became blurred (and remain so in Europe to this day). The monastic communities in the mid- and late-Middle Ages were, in large measure, economic exercises. The monasteries were a blessing to

Christianity and the lifeblood of local cities and towns but also places of rampant financial excess and abuse.

The Reformation was initially about money. Martin Luther's original objection was to the suspect fundraising methods employed to raise the staggering sums required for the construction of St. Peter's Basilica in Rome. Disavowing the deep corruption of the late Renaissance Church, the Reformation divided Western Christianity, leading to five hundred years of controversy and conflict.

Today, all of us have been exposed to parishes that overemphasize money: pushing the need for it and the lack of it while investing a lot of effort in inevitable, intrusive fundraising. It is commonplace to hear of money mismanagement in parishes, dioceses, and even in the Vatican.

And, as churchpeople, we bristle at the idea that money *rules*. We know that *God* rules. We all believe that there is more to life than money. People love their families and friends, country, and core beliefs. They have hopes and dreams they fondly hold, fears and frustrations they carefully manage. As church leaders, we invite people to live out their higher ideals, to follow their better angels. We don't want them to be driven by money or possessions that are fleeting. We want them to work for enduring things money cannot buy—peace and goodwill, grace and truth, but most importantly, a loving relationship with the living Lord. Money cannot ultimately satisfy the human heart, nor does it nourish our souls. As churchpeople, we know all this. And yet . . .

And yet, we have to acknowledge that, as a Church, money is an indispensable tool.

It takes money to do ministry. Churches need money to maintain buildings and properties—costs that keep climbing, especially in parishes saddled with aging facilities and decades of deferred maintenance. There are utility bills and operational expenses that keep coming. Parishes, like every other organization, have administrative costs that never go away.

Increasingly, parishes must (and should) rely on lay staff who must (and should) be paid. Growing your staff takes money too, and growing it could be a strategic necessity. An Evangelical church in our region, with a congregation somewhat smaller than ours, has a staff three times the size of our staff. We currently have three full-time staffers for middle and high school ministry. They have ten. So, guess what? They can offer a lot more for their students than we can.

Churches also need money to maintain and improve the *quality* of ministry. Money, well spent, makes what we do *better*. However aspirational our intentions and lofty our goals, quality and excellence are achieved, in no small measure, with money. The investment of money in our programs and services is part of the *process* of pursuing excellence.

As a church, we absolutely believe in the importance of volunteer ministers. Parishes cannot be healthy, nor can they grow, if parishioners aren't serving (we call them *member-ministers*). But we also believe volunteers work best when they are assisted and supported by the leadership of paid, professional staff. For instance, we have hundreds of leaders who guide our adult small groups. They work for free, but they are recruited, trained, scheduled, and equipped by our director of small groups, Susan. And Susan is paid. When someone is paid for their service, it helps to infuse an organization with a professional mindset firmly footed in accountability.

You need money to staff a volunteer program, and you also need money for the needs of your volunteers. The list can be an extensive one: art supplies for kids' ministries, rain gear for our parking ministers, aprons and caps for our café ministers. Our member-ministers must be fed if they are here at meal times, and drinks and snacks should be available at other times too. And, from time to time, they need to be thanked and at least modestly rewarded. And that takes money too. We have a saying around here that *volunteers aren't free.*

**Father Michael:** Money is also critical to innovation and growth. Recently, we were having a conversation about "Live!"—our online campus, where we live stream all of our Sunday Masses and rebroadcast them at other times. It's our fastest-growing ministry and, I believe, our field of greatest opportunity. As we discussed the program, we learned from our tech team that to take the ministry to the next level we need dedicated cameras for the live feed, in addition to the ones providing the house feed. This would be an additional and not insignificant expense that we weren't even considering and can't currently afford. It would be money well spent, but it's money we just don't have.

This happens all the time in parishes everywhere. If you look around your church, you know well that there are plenty of programs and services you could and want to offer, events and experiences you want to expand, and facilities and technologies you would improve if greater financial resources were available.

There is a balance required. The need for money should not be the *only* factor in our strategic decisions, but it is a *huge* one. God is sovereign. Christ is King. But money is a crucial tool.

# Fact 2: Money Is a Lens

Money clarifies our current values and vision, and it refines our hopes and dreams for the future.

Sometime ago we committed to undertake a capital campaign to build a new sanctuary, which we'll share more about later. We did not decide to build because our community needs another church, nor because we needed a prettier one. Baltimore has all the churches we'll ever need. And if pretty churches made disciples, all those beautiful churches in Europe would be full. There was no need to build if, that is, we were content to provide seats and parking only for our regulars—if we didn't want a wider reach and a greater impact in our community. Nor would we have conducted a capital campaign to painstakingly raise the necessary money. We launched a campaign to build a church that would serve as a compelling platform. And on that platform, we could more successfully reach our community for Christ, by offering empty seats at optimal times.

There were plenty of people who advised against it. Some judged it risky and unnecessary. They were half-right—it was incredibly risky. But a bigger vision necessitated more money. John Maxwell likes to say, "Where there is no vision the people perish. Where there is no money the vision perishes." Our vision must be funded. And the bigger the vision, the more money we'll need to make it come to fruition. The clearer you get about your vision, the more clearly you see the need for money.

Obviously, since money is such a necessary resource, and a limited one, it forces us to set priorities. Out of all the possible options, where will we spend our money? Economics is the study of how people make these decisions. It asks how individuals, families, businesses, organizations, and governments allocate their limited, often scarce resources. In other words, economics is the study of how people deal with scarcity.

> **Tom:** Some time ago, my wife, Mia, and I were reviewing our family budget. This exercise forced us to have an uncomfortably frank discussion on a variety of challenging issues. We realized we needed to talk about our schedule for the month ahead and any extra activities and events that required funding. We acknowledged that we simply had to establish priorities: a long-planned date night away from the kids was reevaluated. Where did we want to go? What did we want to do? How much did we want to spend? Discussing money forced both of us to set priorities.

When we committed to build the new church, there was a whole world of options and opportunities, furniture and finishes, lighting and technology, that we could have pursued and often very much wanted. But we also wanted to bring the project in under budget. And that meant animated conversations and difficult decisions about our priorities.

In the same way, forming and following our parish's budget requires us to keep a critical eye on our *ministry* and just how well it's serving our *mission*. Our priorities as a parish are decided by how we allocate money in our budget. The reality is that we only value what we are committed to invest in financially. If we aren't willing to pay for something, then we don't really care about it—not really. During the Watergate scandal, in order to expose the criminals, reporters Bob Woodward and Carl Bernstein were told by their source to "follow the money." Follow the money, and you will usually come to understand the whole picture, get the full story, and learn what's really going on. Money helps us *see*.

# Fact 3: Money Is a Big Part of the Story of the Bible

Far from a distraction or necessary evil, money is an essential part of the story of the Bible—a big part. When you read the Bible, you realize that it suggests a very different approach to money than most of the world takes. Scripture provides a spirituality of money (which we will be discussing later) as well as practical advice on how to handle it effectively.

The scriptures laud and honor people who build wealth and skillfully handle their financial resources. Think about it: Abraham, Isaac, and Jacob were wealthy men. In fact, they were men of *great wealth*, each successive generation growing in wealth. Much of the story of Genesis is the story of their family's growth in wealth.

And then comes the rags-to-riches tale of Joseph. Rising from slavery and imprisonment, Joseph was eventually commissioned to handle the money and resources of the most powerful nation on earth. He had at his disposal all the storied wealth of the Egyptian Empire. His skill at managing that money saved the empire and made it vastly more powerful. Joseph became the wealthiest man in the world. And generations later when the Jews left Egypt, they left wealthy, laden with treasure they had extracted from their captors.

After meeting with God on Mount Sinai, Moses's first instruction to the Israelites was all about money and giving to God out of their enormous Egyptian loot.

David amassed historic levels of wealth throughout his long reign as king and then, he devoted the last season of his life to running what amounted to a capital campaign to build the Temple of Jerusalem.

Solomon, his son, was even richer, and the Bible goes to some length to describe the depth and breadth of his extravagant wealth.

When the kingdom of Israel fell into the chaos of civil war, it was all about money and the foolish financial policies of the king, Rehoboam. He got himself into trouble because he was greedy. The divided kingdoms of Judah and Israel as described in First and Second Kings were weaker than their enemies because they were *financially* weak, eventually leading to their demise. Later, when it came time to rebuild Jerusalem, the project fell to Nehemiah and Ezra, people who knew how to raise the money to do it.

The book of Proverbs provides an abundance of practical advice about building wealth and avoiding the pitfalls of poor financial management.

- Proverbs speaks of the importance of saving: "Precious treasure and oil are in the house of the wise, but the fool consumes them" (21:20).
- There is a warning against borrowing and going into debt: "The rich rule over the poor, and the borrower is the slave of the lender" (22:7).
- And good accounting practices are encouraged: "Take good care of your flocks, give careful attention to your herds" (27:23).

While Jesus was seemingly not born into wealth, he would have needed some money for daily living. As a carpenter in his early life, he was likely a small business owner whose job included purchasing and pricing, accounting, and billing. During his public ministry, he and his disciples would have needed money to travel about healing, teaching, and preaching the Good News. Jesus turned to and relied on the money and possessions of friends. Lazarus, Martha, and Mary were likely very wealthy. Jesus and the apostles made use of their home and hospitality, and it is reasonable to believe these close friends were funding his work. Some of the disciples, who joined the traveling entourage of Jesus, seem to have been quite wealthy.

The Gospel of John tells us that Judas was in charge of the apostles' common purse used to fund their mission and ministry. There we also learn that his greatest betrayal was financially motivated. He turned on his friends to hide his embezzlement and to profit from the reward associated with Jesus' arrest.

Many of Jesus' parables rely on illustrations involving money and the use of money to help us understand the kingdom of God. Think of the parables of the talents, the unrighteous steward, the unforgiving servant, and the pearl of great price, just to name a few.

One of the regular practices and defining characteristics of the early Church was giving. Generosity and giving proved absolutely necessary to the life of the community from the very beginning of our story. "All who believed were together and had all things in common; they would sell their property and possessions and divide them among all according to each one's need. Every day they devoted themselves to meeting together in the temple area and to breaking bread in their homes" (Acts 2:44–46).

So you might now be thinking, *Doesn't the Bible also tell us that money is bad?* Actually, it doesn't. Nowhere does the Bible suggest there's anything wrong with money.

Jesus never said that money was bad. He did, however, say that it was the greatest competitor for our hearts. He also acknowledged that having great wealth can prove to be a challenge when it comes to entering into his kingdom. But Jesus never suggested it was evil or to be avoided. In fact, it was often a theme in his teaching.

# Fact 4: Money Is a Test

Money creates tension, and we live our lives in this tension. Maybe they don't use money in heaven, but it sure "comes in pretty handy down here, Bub" (as George says in *It's a Wonderful Life*). Perhaps more than any other aspect of our lives, money exemplifies the tension we feel of having both a body and a soul, with practical necessities and spiritual longings.

As author Phillip Yancey wrote in *Money*, "I feel pulled in opposite directions over the money issue. Sometimes I want to sell all that I own, join a Christian commune and live out my days in intentional poverty. At other times, I want to rid myself of guilt and enjoy the fruits of our nation's prosperity. Mostly I wish I did not have to think about money at all."

There are times, both personally and corporately, when it seems as if we're devoting too much attention to money and the finances of our parish. Other times, perhaps, we're definitely not giving it enough attention. And then, of course, there is always the constant chorus of complaint from critics asserting that "all you guys talk about is money." The reality of our circumstances is that we need more of it.

Money brings tension. And while, like Yancey, we may wish we didn't have to think about it at all, God doesn't agree. He wants us to learn to balance our need for money on this earth and its real worth in light of eternity. Living in that tension, we are tested and challenged, and God changes us.

Money tests our character because it requires us to develop a solid work ethic and firm disciplines around the way we handle it. When we work hard to make money or raise it, we come to know the value of a dollar. This is why wise parents don't just give their children whatever they want. They know that earning the money to pay for some of the extras in life helps with character growth. It is also why God doesn't just provide windfalls for our parishes; he wants us to grow to understand how to motivate people to give over time.

Scripture teaches that saving is the wise thing to do. Lavish, selfish, or just plain thoughtless consumption reveals a foolish heart.

We see this truth played out over and over again with lottery winners. After collecting their winnings, the lucky few are more likely to declare bankruptcy within three to five years than the average American. CNBC tells the story of Jack Whitaker who won $315 million in the West Virginia lottery and later wished he had torn up the ticket. He admitted he didn't like the person he had become. The pressure of the money had led to his daughter and granddaughter's drug addictions and overdoses. Many people who receive a windfall of money in one way or another often don't have the character to handle it wisely. This is why Proverbs 13:11 tells us, "Wealth won quickly dwindles away, but gathered little by little, it grows."

Money tests our character: when we get more, and handle it prudently, our character grows along with our wealth. On the other hand, when we are rash or foolish with wealth, we diminish our character along with our bank account. When God gives us money as individuals, or corporately as a parish, it is a test of our ability to be good stewards. Used wisely and well, God can entrust more to us.

Money reveals our character, and it also tests our *trust* in God as a provider. St. Ignatius Loyola wrote, "Work as if everything depends upon you, and pray as if everything depends upon God." The paradox of money is that we are to work for it as if we are all alone and on our own while praying and trusting in God to provide for us.

No matter how much money we have, there are always possible scenarios or potential problems in which *we do not* or *will not* have enough. And if we have a large enough vision for our lives or for our parishes, it will *always* require more money than we have.

Whether we will manage those limited resources in a way that trusts and honors God is a test and a constant one. Over and over and over again, we will face this test. It never goes away.

The test that money represents is ultimately a *spiritual* test. We need money, and giving it away is a vital part of discipleship. God cares about how we meet this test.

# Fact 5: Money Management Is Leadership

As we've studied successful organizations and their leaders, we learned that they all have great and compelling vision. But they also know how to *fund their vision*. For example, both of us attended Loyola University in Baltimore. One long-serving president there, Fr. Joe Sellinger, S.J., was and remains a local legend. He took Loyola from a small commuter college for young men of North Baltimore to a regional leader of national note (as well as a national lacrosse powerhouse). He did many things well, not the least of which was raising a lot of money and wisely investing it in transformative institutional growth and development. People were willing to follow him, in part, because of how he handled money.

The healthiest, growing churches in our country, the ones that are most successfully reaching their communities, all have enormous budgets, even though they're mostly scrappy start-ups. How did they do that? They taught their people to give, and as a result they are able to reach more people.

We learned that serving as pastoral leaders demands that we establish and exercise leadership through stewardship. Money management is leadership. We cannot be the leaders God wants us to be while ignoring the finances of our parish. The Church cannot be the Church God wants it to be if we are not regularly increasing our parish budget and consistently strengthening our stewardship of what we have already received.

The reason our parish faced such daunting financial problems was not because people were ungenerous or could not be inspired to give. Nor was it because the economy was poor or the market was down. The reason our parish was facing financial problems was our own failure in leadership. To turn our finances around, we had to step up and take responsibility.

**Tom:** I had a baseball coach who liked to say, "Don't make excuses; make the plays." (By the way, in this book, whenever there is a sports reference or analogy, you can pretty much assume that part is written by me.)

As leaders, we finally determined to stop making excuses when it came to money and our parish. We decided to do what we could do to grow our finances, so our parish could succeed as God wants us to succeed. We went ahead and took the simple steps necessary to increase our parish budget and, in the process, bring people closer to Christ. First, we had to acknowledge that there was a part of us that had been abdicating responsibility when it came to giving and that we had been blaming the people in the pews instead.

**Father Michael:** After the publication of our first book, *Rebuilt*, we had the privilege of going to Australia and speaking at a conference just outside Sydney. We loved it there. The Australians we met were amazing hosts and wonderfully hospitable to us. Toward the end of the conference, we had a spirited discussion with a young bishop (whom we also really liked, by the way). We argued that, in order for the Australian Church to grow, eventually they'll need to hire more lay staff for their woefully understaffed parishes. We noted that increased staffing necessitates more money, and that would be the critical path moving forward. He objected, saying, "We Australians are cheap blokes. Our people will never give." Since we had only been in the country for all of five days (and he's the bishop, after all) we accepted him at his word. Until . . .

That weekend, we visited Hillsong Church, one of the largest and fastest-growing megachurches anywhere (a real phenomenon in a deeply secularized country). You may be familiar with their music, which is internationally popular and played in churches and on Christian radio stations around the world. Hillsong has several campuses, and we visited two of them. And from both it was clear that these were extremely well-funded churches. Money had been invested in lighting and technology and was evident in the general maintenance of their state-of-the-art facilities, as well as the quality of finishes and furnishings. There had to be money to pay the large, talented staff and amazing musicians we met. We thought, "Someone had to pay for all of this. Someone had to give to make this a reality." Our guess? It was a lot of cheap Australian blokes.

With all due respect to our friend the bishop, an otherwise very effective leader, often the lack of giving and the accompanying budget problems are the result of a lack of effective leadership on our part, not the parishioners' apathy. When we blame people in our pews, we abdicate leadership. Let's not do that.

You don't have to be a financial wizard to improve the financial health of your parish. We're certainly not. But we do have to have a solid awareness and growing understanding of the facts about money, at least when it comes to growing a parish. This book is designed to move from reflection to determination, from paralysis to action, and from resignation to resolve, so that we can address the finances of our parishes and the spiritual lives of our parishioners in a Christ-honoring way.

# 3

# LOSING OUR *WHY* / LOSING OUR WAY
## *5 INSIGHTS WE'VE GAINED*

God's work done in God's way will never lack God's supply.

—HUDSON TAYLOR

**Father Michael:** In my initial year at Nativity, my very first summer, the parish was running behind on its budget for the third time in as many years. And, I might as well add, the deficit developed in an affluent community enjoying a flourishing economy. Frank, the volunteer accountant on staff at the time, came to me with his concerns, which fueled my own. As a first-time pastor, I didn't understand the budget process, and I had no insight into how to raise giving levels or keep spending down. But I felt I had to do something.

My first amateur effort involved publishing, in the weekly bulletin, the budgeted collection alongside the amount actually collected. This was unhelpful. That's because the budget projected a weekly collection based on the average weekly collection of the previous year. But the money didn't come in that way. The first weekend of the month always brought the largest collection (by far) because many people only give once a month. Most other weeks the collection was and still is well below the average, but the parishioners didn't know that and neither did I. So, three or four weeks a month we seemed to be advertising our failure to meet our budget. This tended to discourage some people and annoy plenty of others. It motivated no one.

My next strategy was to begin publishing our weekly bills: payroll, utilities, maintenance. The idea was to educate people on the real costs of running a parish, which definitely needs to be done since too many Catholics are unaware of those costs and used to getting church for free. But the effort began to feel as if we were nagging people to give more (which, admittedly, we were). One Sunday, an annoyed parishioner, armed with that week's bulletin listing that week's bills, waved it in my face, complaining, "We've all got bills." These strategies received so many negative comments that they were eventually abandoned.

In our experience, sharing bills is not an effective strategy for raising money. And, when it comes to sharing any kind of numbers, we learned to be careful. Numbers are funny. Numbers need context. In and of themselves they don't necessarily tell the story you're trying to tell or even any story at all. No one knows whether a number is good, bad, or indifferent unless you give some context. If you're going to share numbers (and consider carefully where and how you do), you have to tell people what the numbers mean and how they should think about them.

Since our initial, halting efforts, we've gained a lot of insights about the why, what, and how of churchmoney . . . well, actually only *five*. But that feels like a lot to us. And here they are.

# Insight 1: We Need Money

We've all heard the knee-jerk complaint: "All the church wants is my money." But the truth is, we need money to do ministry. There is no getting around that fact. In order to fund our ministries, we must, in one way or another, convince people to give us their money. We know that is stating the obvious (over our years of pastoral experience we've developed an amazing grasp of the obvious), but *sometimes* the obvious must be stated.

So the question becomes: How do we get the money we need to fund our ministries?

# Insight 2: Manipulation Works . . . for a While

Fundraising is an exercise in influencing behaviors. Essentially, there are only *two* ways to influence human behavior. The first way is to manipulate it. Manipulation works. It works in the marketplace and is widely used as a business model that can shape financially successful outcomes. Businesses use price, promotions, and peer pressure. They employ novelty and innovation or just plain old-fashioned fear to get people to buy their products, use their services, attend their events, and travel to their destinations. These manipulations can powerfully drive short-term sales and influence immediate results. They are especially effective when it comes to creating a single transaction.

But while manipulation can work in the short term, there is a steep downside to it. It cannot create brand loyalty in the marketplace. More important for our discussion, manipulation will not establish long-term or lasting relationships between customers and consumers. Companies that rely on manipulation as a sales strategy do not develop a loyal consumer base.

Manipulation *does* create stress for both the buyer and the seller. Pressure is on the buyer to constantly find the best deal in an ocean of ads and offers and a world of doubt. Manipulation puts stress on the retailer to constantly create more promotions, new gimmicks, and fresh features. It is a never-ending, no-winning, ultimately exhausting "hamster wheel" of an exercise that weakens organizations.

When it comes to raising money in the not-for-profit world, manipulation *always* yields cash. That's why every charity from the Salvation Army to the Humane Society uses it. The need for money to sustain services and ministries and meet our church budgets creates a powerful, sometimes irresistible temptation to manipulate people to give. And as the *need* escalates, so does that *temptation*. We must openly acknowledge that fact. And we've also got to accept that this temptation will never go away.

There are basically two forms of manipulation in the toolbox of most not-for-profits: guilt and fundraisers.

Guilt can include any of the following:

- peer-pressure: *"Everyone else is giving, so you should too."*
- need: *"This is a cause that demands your support."*
- lack of past support: *"It's about time you do your fair share."*
- public humiliation: *"We dare you not to give."*
- fear: *"There might be consequences to not giving."*

Guilt tactics are ugly. Lock the doors. Demand everyone takes a pledge card. Line by line, instruct them in how to fill it out, in condescendingly belabored detail. And then, stare them down until they do it. That's a great way to get lots of commitments for your fundraiser. Pass the basket with urgent pleas from the pulpit about how desperately support is needed, and however many times you pass it, some people will throw in something. Guilt works (for a while), but it does not encourage loyalty to the parish or love for the Church. And it doesn't make disciples—just increasingly resentful consumers.

And when it comes to guilt, the Church has got the ultimate trump card: we can send you to hell or save you from it.

**Father Michael:** We had a very talented and effective weekend assistant here for a number of years. During one season, when finances were particularly weak, I bemoaned the situation to him privately. To my surprise, at the 10:30 a.m. Mass that day, he let the congregation have it: "Shame on you! Shame on you! This parish deserves better from you." The collection shot up robustly. For exactly one week.

**Tom:** Fundraisers are a form of manipulation as well. In my first few years in youth ministry, I undertook an interminable series of fundraisers to raise money for our youth programs and trips. It's really all I did. And my fundraising approach included a full range of annoying efforts: everything we could think of selling from Christmas wreaths to Easter flowers. All of them were essentially ways to get people to give us money (that they otherwise wouldn't) by manipulating their financial support that we didn't deserve. In the end, these fundraisers left me (and everybody else) beat up and burnt out.

And, of course, we also had raffles. One season we raffled off a new car—at least, we tried. We found ourselves struggling to sell enough tickets to cover the cost of the car itself, much less make any profit. As a result, we kept pushing back the date of the drawing, hoping to sell more tickets. Meanwhile, the car sat in front of our entrance as a big, shiny example of how much we didn't get it.

# Insight 3: Move from *Why* to *How* to *What*

Author Simon Sinek argues that more successful companies start at a place far from manipulation. He refers to this place as the "golden circle." The golden circle is a path or plan that moves from *why* to *how* to *what*. Many companies in their marketing and advertising only share what they sell. For example, they say: "Here is a brand-new computer that has all these cool features. Do you want to buy one?"

On the other hand, the "inspired companies," as he calls them, start with their *why*, their core purpose. Apple communicates, through its advertising and marketing, that they want to challenge the status quo and lift up the power of the individual through technology that is entirely accessible and uber chic. All of their advertising comes back to this core purpose, expressed in every possible way from store design to product packaging. Next, they make the argument that their products are an expression, an incarnation, of their mission and vision. Then, and only then, do they ask, "Do you want to buy one?" In the process, they've also changed the world.

Their *why* leads to *how*, which generates *what* they do. In other words, the company has a mission, which leads to its strategy, which drives its sales. The mission determines their products, their major decisions, and really everything they do as an organization. Sinek argues that the most successful companies have a crystal-clear understanding of their mission. Their business strategies flow from that understanding, and financial success follows.

Another amazing example of this same idea is Southwest Airlines. Southwest began with the aim of democratizing air travel. Founder Herb Kelleher wanted air travel to be available to every American, not just a wealthy few. Over the years, Southwest has developed disciplined and creative strategies that support this core mission. It's *why* for so long they used only one type of plane (one plane meant lower maintenance costs and faster turnover on the ground). It's *why* they don't have assigned seats. It's *why* they push customers to buy online and *why* their rewards program is so easy and simple. It's *why* their staff relies on off-beat humor in their customer relations. It's *why* they only serve two kinds of snacks. Their *why* determines their *how* and their *what*.

# Insight 4: What He *Didn't* Say

When it came to our parish, what was our *why*? We had no idea starting out. Consequently, we had no way of knowing if we were succeeding, or even moving in the right direction—even when we *were* moving in the right direction.

Before Jesus left this earth, he was very clear about the mission and purpose of the Church. He gave us our *why*. The twenty-eighth chapter of Matthew recounts the empty-tomb narrative and what happened after Jesus rose from the dead. Before he ascended into heaven, he gathered the eleven remaining loyal apostles and said, "All power in heaven and on earth has been given to me" (Mt 28:18).

To truly understand this teaching, we have to go all the way back to the book of Genesis. When God created the earth, he gave authority over it to our first parents and said to them, "Fill the earth and subdue it" (Gn 1:28).

God gave humanity power and authority over the earth, but we know what happened next. Our first parents surrendered that authority to the Evil One when they ate the forbidden fruit from the Tree of the Knowledge of Good and Evil. Subsequently, the story of the Old Testament explains God's preparation to win back that authority for humanity—preparation that took generations upon generations to complete.

Finally, at the appointed time, God sent his Son into the world. He worked miracles. He healed people. He preached an amazing message of grace and truth. And then, when his hour came, he entered his Passion. He was beaten, bloodied, mocked, abused and abandoned, crowned with thorns, and then nailed to the Cross. All this he endured in perfect obedience to the will of his Father to give back to humanity the authority it had surrendered in the Garden of Eden.

Then, following his Resurrection, Jesus says to the apostles, "All authority in heaven and on earth has been given to me. Now, guys, I am passing it on to you. I want you to take that authority, and I want you to go. I want you to go and . . ."

Now, think about what he *doesn't* say. He doesn't say: "go and run raffles . . . host spaghetti dinners . . . put parish life on hold for the spring carnival . . . sell stuff in your lobby nobody wants." No, remarkably, he doesn't say any of that. He doesn't even say, "Go and play bingo." Instead he says, "Go, therefore, and make disciples of all nations, baptizing them in the name of the Father, and of the Son, and of the holy Spirit, teaching them to observe all that I have commanded you" (Mt 28:19–20).

That's it. That's our *why*. Our mission is to make disciples, or followers, of Jesus Christ. It sounds so simple. But . . .

# Insight 5: It's So Easy to Lose Our *Why*

Our *why* is entirely straightforward and incredibly simple. It's *simple*; it's just not *easy*. So many people in parish ministry lack focus on the mission of the Church. Some come to believe, or at least act as if, the Church is about protecting the liturgy, defending the Eucharist, or promoting their preferred style of music. Many see their parish as a private club to find fellowship and make friends. Others consider it a refuge from the world, a retreat from contemporary culture. As we recounted in *Rebuilt*, we thought the purpose of the Church was to satisfy religious consumers. In other words, we were lost. When we lose our *why*, we lose our way.

This is true for every area of parish life but especially applicable when it comes to finances. The pressure to make budget, pay staff, fund programs, or, increasingly, just survive can tempt us away from making disciples.

The reality is that the path toward financial health and stability in our parishes is not running away from our mission but toward it. The more we connect money and discipleship, the healthier our church finances will be. Put it this way: if we're successfully attracting the unchurched, getting them on a clear, accessible discipleship path, and equipping them with the steps they need to grow, then we will see an increase in giving from the members of our church.

As C. S. Lewis notes, "Aim for heaven and you will get earth thrown in. Aim for earth and you lose both." When we successfully connect discipleship and giving, the money always follows. When we just aim for money, we miss out on both. This has been our experience. As we slowly came to this insight, we began and continue to see an increase in giving to our parish.

Raising money, in accordance with God's teaching in scripture, as an exercise in discipleship, is a faith journey for parish leaders. Over the last few years, connecting discipleship and money has required us to grow in our faith, forcing us to trust that if we keep pursuing money in God's way, then God would provide. All the earth is the Lord's. It all belongs to him. He has all the money needed to fund our ministries. Focusing on money through the lens of discipleship has helped us come to believe that. In the process, we've experienced God's provision firsthand.

But first, we've got to believe God *wants* to fund his parishes. And guess what? He will. When we are doing God's will, in God's way, God provides the funding.

# Part II

# THE BIBLE, MONEY, AND OUR PARISH

# 4

# JESUS ON MONEY
## *6 LESSONS WE'VE LEARNED*

For where your treasure is, there also will your heart be.

—MATTHEW 6:21

S o, what did Jesus say about money?

**Father Michael:** As uncomfortable as I was about the whole issue of money when I first became pastor, this discomfort was amplified exponentially at the prospect of a capital campaign. The looming campaign was more or less thrust upon us by our archdiocese. Leaders there had decided to run a campaign, giving each parish a goal (read "assessment").

The only way to reach our goal was to run a parish version of the larger campaign. And as long as we were going to all the trouble to do it—so the thinking went at the time—why not raise some money for ourselves? This might make the archdiocesan pitch more attractive to parishioners and leave us with something for all our effort. Our classroom wing was in sad shape after almost forty years of constant use and consistent neglect. We decided to double the goal given by the archdiocese and raise additional money to renovate and modestly expand our classroom space. The goal was thus set at $1 million.

Now, whether that number strikes you as a lot or no big deal, please allow us to emphasize that it was a *very big deal* for our parish—in fact, somewhat overwhelming. Besides, the parish had never run a capital campaign before (ever). For most it was a completely unfamiliar and unwelcome exercise. The very idea that our parish could come up with a sum like that was a source of amazement to most and derision to others.

> **Tom:** Here's what happens when untested leaders (us) set a high goal for their followers (our parishioners). All the naysayers (you don't expect) line up with the critics (you've already got) and proclaim your inevitable failure. Those sitting on the fence begin to jump off to the other side, and potential supporters go wobbly, friends start asking probing questions that suggest doubts, and the staff becomes nervous. Heck, you begin doubting yourself. It is a very uncomfortable position to be in. We moved forward anyway as we really had no choice.

Of course, we did all the requisite things the professional fundraisers say you should do, beginning with hiring a consultant (who quickly proceeded to underwhelm us). The guy only actually showed up a couple of times to instruct us from his tired playbook in a cynical and condescending way, leaving the heavy lifting and hard work to us. We put together a handsome brochure with a clear and compelling case statement, no thanks to our consultant. We sent direct mail pieces to our regular donors as well as potential ones; hosted endless lunches, dinners, and coffees with potential lead givers; and had a big kick-off party for everyone. It was a lot of work and took up tons of time.

> **Father Michael:** Then came the all-important "in-pew" weekend. Parishioners were invited to make their pledge, after which we would definitively know success or failure. I carefully prepared

for my message that weekend, which immediately preceded the time for everyone to fill out their pledge cards. Thus, the homily became the final argument, the closing statement. Focusing on the parish side of the project, we emphasized the argument that seemed to be the most attractive during the campaign: supporting the next generation in their faith (by renovating those classrooms!). And in the smartest move of all, we gathered sample audiences to preview my preaching and give us feedback (a practice that we have come to use whenever we have an important message).

The weekend was a stressful one for sure, during which there were definitely many different emotions stirring in the parish. We felt conflicting emotions ourselves, amplified by the fact that at that point, we simply had no idea how well we were going to do. Here are some of the comments we got that day following Mass:

- "The parish will surprise you, Father; just wait and see." *Why, we wondered, did they think we would be surprised? Was this a forecast of success or one of failure?*
- "I'll make a pledge if you guarantee that 100 percent of my money stays in the parish. Not one cent to the archdiocese." *What kind of guarantee would you like?*
- "Well, I'm afraid you overstepped yourself this time, young man." *"Young man" was said dripping with condescension, though I am always happy to hear that appellation.*
- "I don't think those classrooms look that bad. Kids today are pampered and overindulged." *As if the kids were demanding the renovations.*
- "We should be raising money to give to the poor." *And then you'd finally give?*

Anyway, it was a long weekend as we waited for the final count (by our regular money counters, who were not a hotbed of support for this campaign, by the way). We squeaked by, barely making our goal. But it might as well have been $2 million for the impact it had on the life of the parish. Critics were silenced (at least for a little while), supporters were vindicated, and a first-ever capital improvement to our aging facility signaled a new day.

And it was all because of money. We should not have been surprised. Jesus had a great deal to say about money. In fact, about 15 percent of his recorded words were directed to the topic. Jesus said more on the subject of money than he said about heaven or hell. Jesus said more about money than he said about sex or marriage. Jesus said more about money than he said about the Church.

So, what *did* Jesus say about money? In looking at his teaching, we found he offers six lessons on its proper use.

# Lesson 1: We Are Stewards, Not Owners of Our Money

In parable after parable, Jesus reinforces and expands this teaching from the Old Testament.

In the sixteenth chapter of the Gospel of Luke, Jesus is addressing the topic of the kingdom of God. At face value, that would seem to be a topic far afield of the subject of money. Not so. Jesus says that the kingdom of God can be compared to a rich man who decided to fire his steward because the man mismanaged the master's funds. The steward, knowing he is about to lose his job, decides to radically reduce the debt of the master's debtors to ensure friendship and support in his unemployment. Surprisingly, at the end of the parable, Jesus commends this dishonest servant for his actions.

Many people hear the parable of the dishonest steward and think Jesus is in some way commending dishonesty, but that's not the point. Jesus uses the story to remind his listeners that the money in their possession is only temporary and that they are not the real owners. In Luke 16:11–12, he says, "If, therefore, you are not trustworthy with dishonest wealth, who will trust you with true wealth? If you are not trustworthy with what belongs to another, who will give you what is yours?"

Through this parable, Jesus is clearly teaching that money doesn't belong to us. It belongs to God. We are not owners of the money that passes through our hands. God is. We enjoy a position of great responsibility: we're stewards. Recognizing that we're *his* stewards helps us use money more wisely, which is in our best interest because it brings us expanded responsibility.

Jesus returns to this point again in the parable of the talents in Matthew 25. There, he compares the kingdom of heaven to a man preparing for a journey, assembling his servants, and entrusting to them his property. The master goes away for a long time. How long?

- It was such a long time that the servants probably wondered if the master was ever coming back.
- It was such a long time that they might have wondered if it even mattered how they used the master's money.
- It was such a long time that they may have been tempted to think that the money belonged to *them* and not to the master who was gone.

But the master *did* return. And consider what he did. First, he settles accounts with them. He rewards the two servants who used the money to enlarge his wealth and punishes the servant who did not invest the resources and wasted an opportunity. Here, too, the parable assumes that money and possessions do not belong to us but to God.

In the parable of the rich fool, we meet a man who experiences the good fortune of a windfall. This fortunate fellow enjoys a bumper crop. He makes so much that he can take the rest of his life easy—eat, drink, and be merry. It sounds like the American dream, but it's not God's vision for our lives. Instead, God says, "You fool, this night your life will be demanded of you; and the things you have prepared, to whom will they belong?" (Lk 12:20).

The answer: someone else. All of us face death. The mortality rate in our country, despite all the advances in modern medicine, still hits exactly 100 percent. Death parts us with the money and possessions we have held onto in this life. When the legendary John Rockefeller died, his accountant was asked, "How much did he leave?" The accountant answered bluntly, "All of it."

Jesus relies on the terminology of business and finance. Our relationship with money is exactly parallel to the terms of a bank loan. Money and possessions are on loan to use for a time before they must be given back. And they must be given back with interest. This is a huge point that we must emphasize to the people in our pews. The question of ownership of money and possessions and how we settle that question greatly colors how we use it. If what I've got is *mine*, then I'll have a greater challenge following the teachings of scripture. If it's all mine, then the teachings to give and sacrifice sound like a much bigger imposition. However, if it all belongs to God, then it completely changes the dynamic. Instead of having a closed-grip mentality about money, people can hold it with an open hand. As David recognized when he gave to God, there can be great joy in giving. "For everything is from you, and what we give is what we have from you" (1 Chr 29:14).

A stewardship mentality is also important when it comes to having the right attitude toward money in general. If I am a steward, then when I lose money in the stock market or suffer a financial setback, it doesn't become an emotional defeat as well. If I grow in wealth, then I know that God has given me the money and possessions to accomplish a greater good.

## Lesson 2: Build Treasure in Heaven

Jesus teaches his disciples that money is in our possession temporarily. We only have it in the short term. But it turns out, we can use it in the long term. When it comes to money, Jesus is not against our using it for our own good. In fact, he encourages his friends and followers over and over again to do exactly that. However, our natural instinct is to use money to our long-term disadvantage. We want to use money to fund *our* plans, *our* pleasures, and *our* kingdom.

Jesus knew that because he understood human nature better than anyone. So, he offers us an appealing motivation. "When you give alms, do not let your left hand know what your right is doing, so that your almsgiving may be secret. And your Father who sees in secret will repay you" (Mt 6:3–4).

When we give gifts to those in need or to Christ's Church, and do it quietly so as to win no recognition or reward, God makes us a promise that we will be richly rewarded in eternity. Jesus says over and over again in his teaching that we should use money to build treasure in heaven. While it is impossible to know what that treasure will look like, there is no denying he wants us to do it.

When a rich young man approaches Jesus, and asks him what he is missing, Jesus says, "You are lacking in one thing. Go, sell what you have, and give to [the] poor" (Mk 10:21a). Perhaps the rich young man didn't hear the rest of the statement. He was so attached to his money and possessions that the loss of them was unthinkable. But think about it: Jesus didn't tell the rich young man to give away his possessions for merely altruistic reasons. Instead, Jesus said that in giving to the poor, he wasn't losing out but rather building heavenly reward: "And you will have treasure in heaven; then come, follow me" (Mk 10:21b).

In the Sermon on the Mount, Jesus devotes several teachings entirely to money and possessions. In the midst of that instruction, he says, "Do not store up for yourselves treasures on earth, where moth and decay destroy, and thieves break in and steal. But store up treasures in heaven, where neither moth nor decay destroys, nor thieves break in and steal" (Mt 6:19–20). Turns out Jesus is all for treasure—the kind with lasting value. You can't keep it but you can send it on ahead.

In the parable of the judgment of the nations, Jesus applauds those who use their money and possessions in the way he teaches us to use them—feeding the hungry, clothing the naked, welcoming strangers, caring for the poor, and visiting prisoners. "Then the king will say to those on his right, 'Come, you who are blessed by my Father. Inherit the kingdom prepared for you from the foundation of the world'" (Mt 25:34).

In another place, Jesus says, "Sell your belongings and give alms. Provide money bags for yourselves that do not wear out, an inexhaustible treasure in heaven that no thief can reach nor moth destroy" (Lk 12:33).

Using money to serve God and his purposes brings rewards of lasting value.

# Lesson 3: Money Represents the Greatest Competition God Faces for Our Hearts

Charles Dickens's novel *A Christmas Carol* is a wonderful holiday tale, and, for many, viewing the movie is a beloved annual tradition. No Christmas is complete without it. (Just for the record, the best version remains the original British one with Alastair Sim. Runner up is the made-for-television classic with George C. Scott.) It is an amazing story with much to teach us about the value of loving and giving.

However, there is one disservice the story has done: it has made it difficult for us to spot greed, especially in ourselves. Ebenezer Scrooge is the very personification of avarice. For the sake of money, he sacrifices everything: consideration for others, care for his family, compensation for his employees, even his own comfort. When his only friend and longtime business partner, Jacob Marley, dies, Scrooge coldly takes possession of Jacob's enormous wealth and property—his only emotion being clutching, covetous, grasping greed. In its extreme form, greed is an intense selfishness that can fixate on money, among other things. Watching Scrooge be Scrooge is anything but self-correcting; quite the opposite. We can conveniently absolve ourselves of greed when we see *him* in action.

**Father Michael:** You know, in all the confessions I've heard over the years, I have never heard anyone confess to greed.

**Tom:** To be honest, I've never actually acknowledged greed in confession.

Greed is a very subtle sin, and almost nobody recognizes that they're guilty of it, or even ever thinks about it at all. And yet, obviously, it is undeniably present in our lives and prevalent in our community and culture.

**Tom:** Sometimes it seems that people are born greedy. This thought comes to me often as a parent of seven kids. I once observed an incident with my son Caleb, who was two years old at the time. Caleb had somehow gotten hold of my iPhone. When I realized he'd taken it, I reached to retrieve it. He refused to surrender my phone, petulantly claiming, "Mine!" Eventually, I got it back (I'm bigger). But I thought, "Where does that attitude come from?" Caleb has never worked a day in his life. He didn't buy the phone. He's never bought anything. He doesn't have any money. Everything that Caleb has in this world has been given to him and supplied for him. Not to mention the simple fact that he had no one to call.

As I thought more about this, it occurred to me that each of my seven children seemed to have come into this world with a "mine" attitude. They don't naturally share with each other but are constantly fighting over toys, food, candy, time on the Xbox—anything and everything. If one child is given a gift, they'll jealously guard it from the others. Why is that? What is it in the human condition that makes a lot of us want to grab all we can get and often not truly care whether others have enough?

Self-differentiation? Self-control and assertion? Identity formation? Or is it maybe just greed?

Sometimes it seems not that greed is the exception to the rule, but
rather that greed *is* the rule, the norm in this fallen world. Flawed human
beings are regularly tempted toward greed, and we risk getting stuck there
unless we learn new behaviors. It's a consistent and constant danger with
the risk of harming our hearts. Greed is not heart-healthy and opens the
door to lots of bad stuff such as cynicism, hypocrisy, and dishonesty. It
can alienate us from those around us, and it will, in even mild forms,
distance us from God.

Yet often, greed is seen as a positive attribute to be admired and
emulated. Remember the movie *Wall Street* in which Gordon Gekko
asserts, "Greed is good"? We are naturally repulsed by that statement,
but it really does undergird what many are thinking. Economists argue
that people who pursue more actually drive the economy. Marketing and
advertising ceaselessly remind us of what we don't have but must have in
order to fit in, stand out, or do whatever it is we're told to do. Constant
consumerism comes at us in so many waves that we don't recognize its
dangers. We read in Luke's gospel, as he introduces the parable of the rich
fool, Jesus' teaching to "take care to guard against all greed, for though
one may be rich, one's life does not consist of possessions" (12:15).

This is an astounding statement. But there is a danger of equating
one's money and possessions with one's very identity. Financial misfor-
tune can lead to hopelessness and despair. The evidence is all around us,
all the time. Financial difficulties end friendships and partnerships and
are the leading cause of divorce. A friend of ours, in realizing this truth,
acknowledged, "I just feel better about life when I have money in my
pocket." There is a real danger in equating *net* worth with *real* worth.

**Tom:** With characteristically "brilliant" timing, I bought my current home at the top of the market, right before the housing
bust. Recently, I had hoped the house had recovered enough

value to refinance my mortgage at a lower rate. Until, that is, the broker called me to report that the appraisal came in below my mortgage, and far lower than I expected. For days afterward, I spent sleepless nights feeling bad about my choices, condemning myself for my poor judgment. I felt terrible, even though the house is a handsome one that serves my family well.

The danger of confusing or even equating net worth and real worth can actually get stronger as we get older. When I was younger, I didn't think much about what was in my retirement account, but once I turned forty, that changed. Suddenly, retirement age doesn't feel so far away, but my financial goals look completely out of reach. At this point, I realize I should have made further progress toward those goals. I think of the line from *It's a Wonderful Life*, when Mr. Potter says to George Bailey, "You are worth more dead than alive."

Of course, intellectually, we know this not true for George Bailey or anyone else, but the thought, the emotion, and the temptation to equate the worth of our lives with our net worth lingers. Remember that rich young man who walked away from Jesus? The incident occasioned one of Jesus' most important statements: "Amen, I say to you, it will be hard for one who is rich to enter the kingdom of heaven" (Mt 19:23).

His disciples are shocked; the remark flies in the face of everything they've been taught and what they understand. Nevertheless, he goes on to emphasize his point in a startling analogy: "Again I say to you, it is easier for a camel to pass through the eye of a needle than for one who is rich to enter the kingdom of God" (Mt 19:24).

The competition money presents to our relationship with God almost seems insurmountable. But the next lesson teaches us otherwise.

# Lesson 4: Money Can Move the Human Heart in the Right Direction

In the Gospel of Luke, we read the story of the tax collector, Zacchaeus. In fact, he wasn't just *any* tax collector but the *chief* tax collector and, as a result, a very wealthy man. The only reason a man would choose to be a tax collector was love of money. Such officials were considered traitors to their country and outcasts from their faith. The Jewish people detested their behavior because they collected money for the Roman oppressors.

Tax collectors actually had to purchase their positions because these jobs were extremely lucrative and much sought after. They were assigned to collect a prescribed tax for Rome, but then they could add any amount they wanted over and above that tax for their own benefit. It was entirely within their discretion to exact unfair or even exorbitant amounts, and they had the power of the Roman army behind them. This led, in turn, to widespread corruption.

Tax collectors and sinners were following Jesus because people who were nothing *like* him *liked* him, and this was a source of scandal to religious Jews. Even the gospel writers were so astounded that tax collectors were following Jesus that they chose to acknowledge them apart from every other kind of sinner.

Zacchaeus had a pile of money, that's certain. But as much as he had, it wasn't enough. He wasn't satisfied. Obviously, he was lonely and alone; probably, he was ridiculed and reviled. All of his money simply wasn't enough. He wants something more, but more of what? He goes out of his way—very much out of his way—just to get a glimpse of Jesus. In fact, we're told in Luke 19:4, "He ran ahead and climbed a sycamore tree in order to see Jesus, who was about to pass that way."

In that day, wealthy, Middle Eastern men didn't do that—they simply didn't run. It was considered deeply undignified, something only children or slaves would do. But Zacchaeus so badly wants to see Jesus that he does it anyway. He runs *and* climbs a tree.

Still more unexpected, Jesus stops at that very spot. And most shocking of all, he invites himself to dinner at Zacchaeus's house. Of all the people he could have eaten with in Jericho, of all the people who would have loved to welcome him, Jesus chooses the greedy, crooked tax collector. Zacchaeus receives him with joy; it is a moment of conversion. And how does Zacchaeus mark this moment? He says to Jesus, "Behold, half of my possessions, Lord, I shall give to the poor, and if I have extorted anything from anyone I shall repay it four times over" (Lk 19:8).

Zacchaeus, who loves money, has a change of heart after meeting Jesus. He discovers a new love. He gives half his fortune to the poor and promises to repay more than he has stolen from others. Jesus responds, "Today salvation has come to this house" (Lk 19:9).

Zacchaeus's resolution to share his fortune with the poor and make restitution to those he defrauded was the sign of his profound repentance. In turn, it was precisely this resolution that disposed him to God's saving grace. When we give our money as God asks us to give, we open our hearts to receive God's strength and grace. In Matthew 6:21 Jesus teaches, "Where your treasure is, there also will your heart be."

Your heart automatically follows your money. If you invest in a company, their performance starts getting your attention. When you buy a new house or car, it takes a part of your heart. Start paying fitness-center fees, and you're likely to exercise more. And if you bought season tickets, you are absolutely going to the game, no matter how badly the team is doing.

**Tom:** I see this with my kid's activities. My older boys were attracted to the martial arts, so they enrolled in a Taekwondo program. I subsequently spent a good deal of money and, as a consequence, became very interested in both their attendance and their progress. Now, I make sure they get to class. And when, from time to time, they don't want to go (because they're kids and that is how kids are), it actually hurts my heart.

Our hearts tend to follow our money. This isn't in itself good or bad, but it is a reality that Jesus observed. And since our hearts will follow our money, then it makes sense to invest our money in places where we want our hearts to go. If you want to have a heart for your parish, then start giving your money there. If you want to grow in charity for the poor, give there.

While money can be a problem for the human heart, we can correct it by using it to build God's kingdom instead of our own.

## Lesson 5: Pay Your Taxes

All three synoptic gospels tell us that Jesus was questioned about paying taxes to the Roman emperor in an attempt to entrap him. Matthew explains that the trap was set by an alliance of the Herodians (essentially secular Jewish allies of the Roman client-kings) and the Pharisees (the orthodox religious leaders). Typically, these two factions were at war with one another. But they both wanted to destroy Jesus. The Greek word in Matthew for "trap" refers to a hunting term and denotes the way you would trap an animal. Matthew's gospel tells us, "They sent their disciples to him, with the Herodians, saying, 'Teacher, we know that you are a truthful man and that you teach the way of God in accordance with the truth. And you are not concerned with anyone's opinion, for you do not regard a person's status. Tell us, then, what is your opinion: Is it lawful to pay the census tax to Caesar?'" (22:16–17).

First, the Herodians transparently flatter Jesus, aiming to lower his defenses. Recognized and revered as a truth teller, he will then reveal what he really thinks about the tax. If Jesus says he is against it, then the Herodians would charge him with inciting rebellion and opposing the rule of Rome. If he supports the tax, he'll lose popularity with the people. (As an aside, this is a good reminder for church leaders that we need to be wise with our words and aware of the motivation behind people's questions.)

The tax they are asking about was a poll tax levied on men from puberty through the age of sixty-five. Constantly and cruelly, the tax reminded the Jewish people that they were subjected to Roman rule. The money went straight into the Roman emperor's coffers. The Jewish people were funding his unbridled power, extravagant luxury, and decadent lifestyle as they eked out an existence in poverty and oppression.

Furthermore, the tax had to be paid with a Roman coin that bore the engraving of the emperor and had on it the inscription "divus et pontifex maximus," which translates "god and highest priest" (literally, "high bridge" connecting Romans to the divine). So, the tax represented an insult and offense to the Jewish people not only politically but religiously as well. The coin was an affront to the First Commandment, and a sacrilege to the whole of Jewish faith.

Matthew's gospel continues, "Knowing their malice, Jesus said, 'Why are you testing me, you hypocrites? Show me the coin that pays the census tax.' They handed him the Roman coin" (22:18–19). By producing the coin, the Pharisees are exposed as artless hypocrites. They themselves relied upon the coin in their own transactions, so their questioning was just a matter of sophistry.

Jesus counters: "'Whose image is this and whose inscription?' They replied, 'Caesar's.' At that he said to them, 'Then repay to Caesar what belongs to Caesar and to God what belongs to God.' When they heard this they were amazed" (Mt 22:20–22). Little wonder. His answer is one of the most brilliant in the whole history of human discourse, fielding their question in a way that amazes and astonishes his opponents. Entirely avoiding their trap, Jesus leaves them simply disarmed. He can neither be accused of inciting rebellion nor of contradicting God's claim on our hearts.

When he says, "Give to Caesar what belongs to Caesar," he is unequivocal. And what was true in ancient Rome is true in contemporary society. Governments produce coinage, and then demand it back through taxes that come in various forms. Jesus' teaching is clear that we are to respect political authority when it comes to paying taxes.

No one likes it. Often taxes are not fairly collected, nor is the money always properly used. We can debate the point all we want, easily finding flaws with the tax system that seem to exempt us from cooperation. It is certainly within our rights to work the system to our advantage, identify as many deductions and exemptions as we might invoke, or hire a team of accountants to do it for us. Within the limits of the tax law we can follow Jesus' own example of shrewdness in dealing with the Herodians and the Pharisees. *However*, the point is working *within the limits of the law*.

Some people argue against paying taxes on moral grounds. Their hearts are pure. They thoughtfully resist, arguing that the government uses money to wage war or fund unjust or immoral programs. However, Jesus' challenge to the Pharisees seems to disallow such a position. Of course, we should do what we can to combat evil, but withholding taxes is not one of them. They may want to make it a moral issue, but actually it's just a financial one.

> **Tom:** Some people cheat on their taxes just because they can get away with it. They don't use morality as a cover; they use convenience. Recently, I was listening to *The Dave Ramsey Show* on the radio, and a woman called into the program. She wanted to hire a full-time nanny. Her plan was to pay cash, under the table, to avoid Social Security taxes. Ramsey discussed some ways she could legitimately get around paying the tax. If she hired a couple of nannies who worked less than full-time, then they would be responsible for paying their own taxes. But when it came to avoiding paying the legal taxes, he said to the woman, "That's not who you want to be."

> **Father Michael:** Cheating on taxes is a huge deal in our culture. On several occasions I have referred to the practice in my preaching, evoking gasps from my congregation. But paying your taxes is just part of the honesty and transparency God wants reflected in our use of money.

# Lesson 6: Don't Worry about Money

We need money because it is a medium of exchange through which we can meet our needs, fulfill our desires, and basically live our lives. And since we *need* money to meet our needs, there is a very reasonable and real danger of worrying about whether we'll have enough. As our responsibilities grow, our worries will grow in tandem.

**Tom:** Raising a family with bills to pay and mouths to feed brings anxiety. The possibilities of an illness or injury bringing financial ruin to a family or a storm destroying one's house in a matter of minutes are scary things to think about. Real anxiety can come from needing a new car. Even navigating the extra expenses of the Christmas holidays or a summer vacation is stressful. As a result, I find myself worried.

**Father Michael:** In becoming a pastor I was surprised (and unprepared) to find myself in the role of a small business owner. As such, I have employees who are relying on me for their livelihood. Recognizing that raising the money to pay them was and is ultimately my responsibility was bracing. And if things were not going well, or we had a bad week, I got worried. Even a one-week, below-budget collection can bring stress and tension.

Worry denotes pain. The origin of the word *worry* means "to choke." Jesus knows that any worry can choke the joy of life out of us. He understands we are especially prone to worry about our finances and that it can become an obstacle not only to joy but to having a relationship with God. He says, "Therefore I tell you, do not worry about your life, what you will eat [or drink], or about your body, what you will wear. Is not life more than food and the body more than clothing?" (Mt 6:25).

First-century Jews worried about basic necessities. They had to, as most lived their lives on the cusp of what for us would look like deep poverty. Many people today still do. For others of us, especially in suburban communities, that isn't our major concern. Some of us have plenty of everything, yet we still worry about money. We worry if we'll have enough to pay for our kids' educational needs. We worry about maintaining our standard of living and continuing to afford our guilty pleasures. We worry if we've saved enough for our retirement and eventual health-care costs. We worry we'll outlive our money. Our culture is proof that there is no amount of money that can take away our worry for it.

And yet, Jesus says *not to worry* because your life is about more than physical needs or even deep desires. Your life is about the health of your heart, the care of your soul, the life of your mind, and the strength of your relationships.

Then, he says something that sounds a little idealistic, a shade condescending, depending on your point of view. He says, "Look at the birds in the sky; they do not sow or reap, they gather nothing into barns, yet your heavenly Father feeds them. Are not you more important than they?" (Mt 6:26). Jesus reminds his audience that God the Father, in a way unknown to us, provides for the birds of the air, even though they don't work and plan like we do. He continues, "Why are you anxious about clothes? Learn from the way the wild flowers grow. They do not work or spin. But I tell you that not even Solomon in all his splendor was clothed like one of them. If God so clothes the grass of the field, which grows today and is thrown into the oven tomorrow, will he not much more provide for you, O you of little faith?" (Mt 6:28–30).

When it comes to our need for money and possessions there is a spiritual component. That's why money is a spiritual issue, calling forth trust in God. So, Jesus says, "Do not worry and say, 'What are we to eat?' or 'What are we to drink?' or 'What are we to wear?' All these things the pagans seek. Your heavenly Father knows that you need them all" (Mt 6:31–32). Pagans worry about their needs because they believe in gods that are not personal. But our Christian faith teaches that we have a heavenly Father who knows our needs and wants to meet them. Seek God and his kingdom, and your other needs will be addressed—at least in a mysterious way we don't understand (and might not even recognize).

The order is very important. We don't get our needs met and then trust God. We trust God by seeking his kingdom first. This goes to the very heart of this book.

Don't make God your safety net or backup financial plan. Seek God and his plan for your parish *first*. Then, and only then, will he fund your mission and vision.

So, Jesus' teachings on money are as follows:

- You are a steward, not an owner of your money.
- Build treasure in heaven through your good stewardship.
- Be on guard against greed.
- Use money to direct your heart toward God.
- Pay your taxes.
- Don't worry.

Then, once you get all this down, you can move on to living out God's guide for giving.

# 5

# GOD'S GUIDE
# FOR GIVING
## *5 RULES WE TRY TO LIVE BY*

Money is a bad master but a great servant.

—FRANCIS BACON

n the thirty-fifth chapter of Sirach we read, "Do not appear before the Lord empty-handed, for all that you offer is in fulfillment of the precepts. The offering of the just enriches the altar: a sweet odor before the Most High. The sacrifice of the just is accepted, never to be forgotten. With a generous spirit pay homage to the Lord, and do not spare your freewill gifts. With each contribution show a cheerful countenance, and pay your tithes in a spirit of joy. Give to the Most High as he has given to you, generously, according your means" (vv. 6–12).

**Father Michael:** At no time during my seminary career or priestly formation did the topic of giving ever come up. Not once. It was raised only a single time in my seminary internship—here at Nativity, by the way (I never got very far in life!). The pastor was reluctant to talk about it, so he didn't talk about it. His approach to church giving was basically to pass the basket and hope for the best. One particular year, the wishful thinking approach wasn't working well at all, and the parish was running a deficit. So the pastor asked the parish accountant to calculate what we needed weekly from each registered household in order to break even. Behind his question was the absurd assumption that every parish household would give and give at the same level. The answer came back: eight dollars a week. And that weekend, that's exactly what he announced to the congregation: "All I want from each family is eight dollars a week. That's your fair share."

Of course, the people who weren't giving anything remained unmoved. But the unintended consequence of his announcement was to permit, even persuade, people who were giving more than eight dollars per week to give less. Collections actually decreased because of this exercise in collecting fees. It did not raise givers—at least not in the way the Bible teaches us to give.

Besides, this was an exercise in collecting fees, not raising givers . . . at least not giving as the Bible teaches us how to give.

Over and over again, Jesus teaches us that we are to give money away. And we need to be willing to part with it for two reasons, which are in our best short-term and long-term interest. In the short term, giving grows our hearts in an immediate kind of way: it feels good. In the long term, it builds treasure in heaven. Yet there are still important questions about giving to be tackled: *Where* are we supposed to give? *How* are we supposed to give?

Here are five rules we try to live by, based on the teachings of the Bible.

# Rule 1: Give as an Act of Worship

Over and over again, the Bible teaches that making an offering to God is an essential act of worship.

- In Genesis, Cain and Abel bring their offerings before the Lord. Cain becomes murderously envious because God looks on Abel's generous gift with favor and rejects his half-hearted one.
- After the flood, the very first thing Noah does is build an altar to the Lord and make a burnt offering in thanksgiving.
- Abraham, after a great victory over his enemies, offers a tenth of all he has to the priest Melchizedek.
- Moses commands giving God worship offerings as part of the code of law he establishes.
- David spends the last portion of his reign teaching the people about giving to God, as part of his fundraising project to build the Temple.
- Hezekiah, in rededicating the Temple, does so, in part, through worship offerings from the whole of the people.

Jesus never explicitly taught people to give as an act of worship, because he didn't have to. It was ingrained in the culture in which he lived and enshrined in the Law of Moses, which he came to fulfill.

# Rule 2: Give in Your Place of Worship as an Act of Worship

In Mark's gospel we read: "When [Jesus] was in Bethany reclining at table in the house of Simon the leper, a woman came with an alabaster jar of perfumed oil, costly genuine spikenard. She broke the alabaster jar and poured it on his head" (14:3).

Jesus was attending a formal dinner party when it was interrupted by an uninvited visitor. She broke an expensive jar of costly oil, shattering it completely to render it useless. Her gift was wholehearted, uncompromising, and, evidently, quite generous.

The other guests at the dinner party didn't welcome the woman's dramatic interruption, nor did they appreciate her extravagant worship offering. Instead, "there were some who were indignant. 'Why has there been this waste of perfumed oil? It could have been sold for more than three hundred days' wages and the money given to the poor'" (Mk 14:4–5).

The value of the oil was roughly equivalent to the annual wages of the average laborer. Some scholars suggest the oil was a family heirloom, which could have served as the woman's marriage dowry. That she lavished this treasure in worship of Jesus was shocking. Immediately, she became the source of criticism born of jealousy by those less generous.

Notice how this incident reflects the same values in giving we learn about in the story of the widow's mite. On that occasion, Jesus is watching as worshipers make their offering at the Temple, and he is most impressed with the modest gift of a poor woman. Like that woman with the perfumed oil, the widow makes a quite significant worship offering. In both cases, Jesus alone recognizes the implication and importance of the sacrifices.

> **Father Michael:** Here's an argument often made when it comes to giving in your place of worship: the money could be given to the poor, as we read in Mark 14:5.
>
> Of course we should give money to the poor. We're not suggesting otherwise. But we have noticed that oftentimes people who make this argument aren't actually interested in helping the *poor*; they just don't want to give to *us*. Giving to the poor can become a red herring to distract from the truth of their hearts.

We see this kind of objection to giving in the Bible story of the woman with the alabaster jar. Some gathered at table with Jesus and his disciples were indignant that the woman anointed Jesus with perfumed oil, which would have been quite costly, saying she could have sold it and given the money to the poor. In the midst of their revelry, it's unlikely they were genuinely concerned about the poor. It's just as likely that they resented their meal being interrupted. Perhaps they also envied the honor extended to Jesus or the attention the woman may have received.

But Jesus responds in what was probably an unexpected way: "Let her alone. Why do you make trouble for her? She has done a good thing for me. The poor you will always have with you, and whenever you wish you can do good to them, but you will not always have me" (Mk 14:6–7). While Jesus definitely encourages giving to the poor elsewhere, in this instance, he honors the woman for giving in her place of worship *instead* of giving to the poor. The dining hall becomes her place of worship as she makes her offering to God there.

Mark intentionally doesn't name the woman, because he invites everyone to identify with her and do as she did.

# Rule 3: Tithe

"The payment of tithes is due to God and those who refuse to pay, usurp the property of another. Those who withhold them or hinder their payment shall be excommunicated, nor be absolved of this crime until full restitution is made" (Council of Trent).

In the second book of Samuel, King David is planning a worship ceremony to the Lord, so that a plague may be withdrawn from his people. Araunah, who owned the place where the altar was to be built, proposed to bequeath all of the necessary worship offerings to the king. Instead, David establishes an important principle, insisting on purchasing the offering. He says, "I cannot sacrifice to the LORD my God burnt offerings that cost me nothing" (24:24).

For worship to be worship, it must cost us something.

A tithe is the gift of 10 percent of what one has or earns, which is given to honor God. Counted in the tithe are all of our gifts in our place of worship as an act of worship. Tithing was established as the consistent standard for worship giving throughout the Bible, beginning in Genesis. Later, Jesus himself explicitly addresses tithing and commends it.

The third chapter of Malachi gives perhaps the clearest picture of the importance of the tithe. God says to the people, "Since the days of your ancestors you have turned aside from my statutes and have not kept them. Return to me, that I may return to you, says the LORD of hosts" (Mal 3:7). God tells the Israelites that he had long ago established a law that they consistently failed to follow. That failure created a gap in their relationship with God, but not, it turns out, an unbridgeable one.

Then, the Israelites ask a good question, "Why should we return?" God responds, "Can anyone rob God? But you are robbing me! And you say, 'How have we robbed you?' Of tithes and contributions!" (Mal 3:7–8). God considers tithing his due. He equates denying him the tithe to theft.

On the other hand, God promises: "Bring the whole tithe into the storehouse, that there may be food in my house. Put me to the test, says the LORD of hosts, and see if I do not open the floodgates of heaven for you, and pour down upon you blessing without measure!" (Mal 3:10). God tells the Israelites to test him on exactly this point. And when they do, putting his teaching in action, they will see his protection and provision over the whole of their lives, including their finances.

Notice where God tells them to bring the tithe: to the storehouse. The storehouse was a dedicated room in the Temple for storing tithed grain. In other words, the tithe would have been brought directly to the place of worship. It was intended to support the Temple and the people who served there.

When it comes to tithing, many people conveniently argue that this is an Old Testament idea that has been done away with in the new covenant. They contend Jesus abolished it in the same way that he made all foods clean or healed people on the Sabbath. However, Jesus states in the

Sermon on the Mount, "Do not think that I have come to abolish the law or the prophets. I have come not to abolish but to fulfill. Amen, I say to you, until heaven and earth pass away, not the smallest letter or the smallest part of a letter will pass from the law, until all things have taken place" (Mt 5:17–18). Throughout his ministry, Jesus' enemies accused him of all manner of offenses, including breaking the Sabbath. But no one ever once accused him of not tithing. Jesus never abolished the tithe or even ever suggested it was no longer applicable to Christians. He consistently affirmed the teachings of the Hebrew scriptures. He did not come to repeal or replace them but to renew and restore them.

Elsewhere, Jesus says to the Pharisees, "Woe to you, scribes and Pharisees, you hypocrites. You pay tithes of mint and dill and cummin, and have neglected the weightier things of the law: judgment and mercy and fidelity. [But] these you should have done, without neglecting others" (23:23). Here, while visiting the Temple courts, Jesus goes on nothing less than a tirade against the scribes and Pharisees. It is a scathing rebuke of their poor leadership. Yet right in the middle of his intense criticism, he acknowledges their tithes. He explicitly commends the Pharisees for tithing, really the only positive observation he ever makes about them.

# Rule 4: Give Beyond the Tithe

In Mark's gospel we read, "[Jesus] sat down opposite the treasury and observed how the crowd put money into the treasury. Many rich people put in large sums. A poor widow also came and put in two small coins worth a few cents" (12:41–42). This took place a few days before Jesus' Passion. Think about that: Just days before he died, only hours left to live, how did Jesus choose to use his time? He sat down in front of the treasury.

The treasury refers to the thirteen trumpet-shaped donation chests that stood in the Temple precincts. It was easy to know what people put in those chests because they were made of metal and people deposited metal coins into them. So, when contributions were made, they were noisy. And the larger the donation, the more noise it made. Jesus sat down *and* listened. It wasn't accidental; it was a deliberate decision.

Often, parishioners will contend that God doesn't care about or even notice what they do with money at church, but clearly Jesus did. He was watching and listening. And he not only noticed, but he evaluated their giving levels, and then commented on them: "Calling his disciples to himself, he said to them, 'Amen, I say to you, this poor widow put in more than all the other contributors to the treasury'" (Mk 12:43).

Widows often lived in poverty since they couldn't inherit their husband's estate or own property themselves. If they didn't have a son to care for them, they often descended into destitution. Jesus doesn't look to the actions of wealthy donors as a lesson in giving for his disciples. He turns to this woman who is poor. And Jesus says something truly astounding—he says that she gave *more* than the rest.

And that statement that she gave "more" is preceded with the imperative "Amen," a solemn assertion Jesus used when he wanted his disciples to grab hold of an important truth. In fact, he used the expression with great purpose in the biblical accounts of the Last Supper as he introduced his disciples to the mystery of what became for us the Eucharist. In Mark's story of the poor widow's contribution, Jesus relies on "Amen" before instructing them on the truth about giving money. Jesus says the widow gave *more* than all the rich people who had put money into the treasury. On the surface, it sounds like utter nonsense. Clearly, in sheer numbers, the rich gave more money. However, Jesus is trying to encourage the disciples and, by extension, all of us to see as God sees. In God's view, according to God's economy, the *percentage* is far more important than the actual *amount*. This is why Jesus says, "For they have all contributed from their surplus wealth, but she, from her poverty, has contributed all she had, her whole livelihood" (Mk 12:44). The wealthy whom Jesus observed at the Temple gave from their surplus, so it cost them nothing. The widow revealed her trust in God by giving from her subsistence. It cost her everything.

This is precisely why, at our parish, we are extremely reluctant to describe anyone's gift as generous. Generosity is certainly a value and virtue we must promote for parishioners. We want them to grow in generosity, but we usually don't know when someone is actually being generous. Admittedly, sometimes we have a hunch. In our capital campaign, we had a sense of the people who had really stretched and sacrificed to give. But we didn't know for sure. We nearly never do, so we don't make this designation casually or quickly.

Jesus is clear that to honor God, we are to give from our substance, even if that means giving beyond the tithe. The widow gave "more" because she gave more than the tithe.

To be honest, if someone of modest means approached us with the intention of donating all of their money, we would probably try to talk them out of it. That's not what Jesus did. He could have interrupted this woman's offering with a very reasonable argument. "Your gift is unnecessary. God doesn't need your money. I've been watching for a while, and the wealthy have provided plenty. So, just hold on to your money." Jesus didn't say any of that to her. Why not? Because he didn't want to rob her of the honor she would receive before God for her gift.

> **Tom:** There is a freedom in being able to give money away that is above the tithe. I experienced that freedom a few years ago. I was on vacation at the beach with my family. When I went to Mass, I felt I was exempt from making any kind of offering because I already give to Nativity and I'm a tither. Besides, I didn't even like the parish I was attending. They actually played canned music, and not only that, but it was really bad canned music. I certainly didn't want to give to them.
>
> God had different plans. I kept hearing a message that I should give. When I relented, I started asking, "How much?"
>
> "All of it. Everything in your wallet."
>
> "Everything?"
>
> "Everything."

Truth be told, I had no idea what was in my wallet. I couldn't remember exactly when I had last gone to the ATM. With seven kids, money on vacation can be tight. As the basket was passed toward me, I took a deep breath, pulled out my wallet, and grabbed all the cash that was in there. It amounted to a total of fourteen dollars. That was it. I had been arguing with God over fourteen dollars. And yet, at the same time, it was much more than that. It was an act of trust on my part; and later I saw God's reward, as far more came back to me over the course of that vacation. At least for that moment, I could associate with the poor widow. I felt that I had pleased God by giving all I had in my wallet—even if it was so little.

When it comes to dollars and cents, the *amount* can be deceiving. Sometimes, people can make a gift that, in light of their financial situation, is very small. However, that same gift may be significant considering where their heart is when it comes to money.

**Father Michael:** Several times over the years, parishioners have asked to meet with me to make what they suggested was a substantial gift to the parish. Surprisingly, on some of those occasions, we received what struck us as modest amounts of money, especially in light of the donor's standard of living. Yet, what we were witnessing was a significant spiritual step. Of course, we have to challenge them to keep growing in their giving, but we also have to acknowledge that dollar amounts don't always tell the whole story.

The tithe isn't a ceiling; it's more like the ground floor, but oftentimes people are starting in the basement.

# Rule 5: Give to the Poor

Jesus didn't teach about giving in your place of worship very often, because he didn't really have to. However, he talked about giving to the poor all the time. One of the principle ways Christ followers give is by donating to the poor.

The first place Jesus teaches giving to the poor is in the Sermon on the Mount. "When you give alms . . ." (Mt 6:2). Here Jesus assumes that his followers will give. He doesn't say, "*If* you give," but "*When* you give." Alms were a means of helping the poor on a weekly or regular basis.

Then Jesus goes on to teach disciples *how* to give: "Do not blow a trumpet before you, as the hypocrites do in the synagogues and in the streets to win the praise of others. Amen, I say to you, they have received their reward" (Mt 6:2). In Luke's gospel the lesson continues: "Do not be afraid any longer, little flock, for your Father is pleased to give you the kingdom. Sell your belongings and give alms. Provide money bags for yourselves that do not wear out, an inexhaustible treasure in heaven that no thief can reach nor moth destroy" (Lk 12:32–33). Jesus' lesson on giving is not as simple or as radical as just getting rid of everything. Instead, he is talking about leveraging our possessions to help the poor.

Since God is already going to share with us the treasures of the kingdom, there is nothing to worry about, and there's actually no risk in giving away our possessions. Jesus paints a vision that money and possessions are of diminished significance in the light of eternity. Prioritizing giving to the poor in your financial planning is of much greater strategic value than saving material wealth for yourself.

In the twenty-fifth chapter of Matthew, Jesus promises the righteous that they will inherit the kingdom prepared for them by his Father. Why? Because of their assistance to him in his own poverty when he was hungry, thirsty, or imprisoned. The righteous themselves wonder where and when they did that. He assures them it was each and every time they assisted those in need.

In another place, Jesus attends a banquet at the house of a disciple, and he instructs his host *not* to invite anyone to a banquet with the means to return the invitation. He says, "Rather, when you hold a banquet, invite the poor, the crippled, the lame, the blind; blessed indeed will you be because of their inability to repay you. For you will be repaid at the resurrection of the righteous" (Lk 14:13–14).

Another place where Jesus teaches about giving to the poor is in the parable of the rich man and Lazarus. In a sobering tale, he makes the point that it is no excuse to claim ignorance of the poor or lack of knowledge about their needs. The rich man didn't directly do anything against Lazarus; he simply neglected him. He was too immersed in his privileges and pleasures to notice the poor man's needs. Clearly, the parable underscores our responsibility in the face of suffering and want. And the implication is that our responsibility actually increases with our physical proximity to poverty. The parable especially challenges all of us in the Western world—where we can so easily become tethered to technology, enslaved to unmanageable schedules, and dependent on our creature comforts that we don't even consider the poor.

Jesus' instruction on giving to the poor is clear:

- Disciples give to the poor.
- Money must be used to do that.
- The poor can present themselves in many different ways.
- There is no excuse for being ignorant of the poor.

Jesus does not, however, address many of the questions and concerns that can slow us down and trip us up when it comes to giving: What are the right charities to give to? What about people who take advantage of others' giving? When is it harmful or counterproductive to give money to someone? To be sure, these are important concerns and considerations. They just shouldn't get in the way of our giving.

Evidently, given the Lord's uncompromising, unambiguous instruction, when in doubt, we are to *give*. Giving is how we grow as disciples, but that's not all. It turns out there is a connection between giving and church growth.

# 6

# GIVING AND CHURCH GROWTH
## *10 PRINCIPLES WE'VE ADOPTED*

Money is like manure; it's not worth a thing unless it's spread around encouraging young things to grow.

—THORNTON WILDER, *THE MATCHMAKER*

**Father Michael:** When I came to Nativity, I found it to be a suburban church in an affluent community where the weekend attendance and the membership were in decline. It was astounding, but undeniable. In what was already a twenty-year trend, the church was losing fifty to sixty people annually. That's not necessarily noticeable the first or second year. But in twenty years, that's one thousand people. The parish was also running small but uncomfortable and surprising deficits.

Of course, what we didn't understand at the time was that our situation was part of a mega trend experienced by parishes everywhere due to myriad and complex new realities in our culture as well as in the larger Church. We also failed to recognize the hardwired connection between church growth or decline and giving. But it's in the Bible.

All four gospels present Jesus' teachings on money, and then the rest of the New Testament goes on to describe how the early Church applied those teachings. In the Acts of the Apostles and the epistles, we meet communities of Christ followers who made Jesus not only the Lord of their hearts, but the Lord of their finances. In the process, the Church grew— exponentially. These two things are not unrelated. It turns out people care about what they invest in. Here are ten principles we've adopted from studying the earliest Christian communities as the Bible reveals them.

# Principle 1: The Church Grows by Inviting God into Its Finances

In the Letter of James, we read, "Come now, you who say, 'Today or tomorrow we shall go into such and such a town, spend a year there doing business, and make a profit'—you have no idea what your life will be like tomorrow" (4:13–14). James specifically criticizes those who make assumptions about the future of their money before inviting God into their plans.

The mentality James is critiquing and criticizing runs deep in much of our consumerist spending in the United States. It is a type of thinking that leads to deep debt and is behind the deficit spending of our government leaders, reckless speculation on Wall Street, and the overspending of many of our fellow citizens. It happens in churchworld too. Assuming future income often leads to purchases that we cannot afford and foolish financial choices we later regret. Healthy spending habits stay focused on the present and what God has already provided, rather than making assumptions about what will be in the future. This is why James goes on to say, "Instead you should say, 'If the Lord wills it, we shall live to do this or that'" (4:15).

Scripture is not averse to financial planning. The admonition is against assuming that we'll enjoy financial success in the future and living our lives today based on that assumption. We are to invite God into our current spending habits and financial planning now, assuming that what he has provided today is an indication of how he wants us to live. In the process, the Church will grow because God honors and rewards this attitude.

# Principle 2: The Church Grows by Identifying Greed as Idolatry

We've already considered the dangers of greed as a principal obstacle to a relationship with God. But in his Letter to the Colossians, Paul goes even further to identify greed as idolatry: "When Christ your life appears, then you too will appear with him in glory. Put to death, then, the parts of you that are earthly: immorality, impurity, passion, evil desire, and the greed that is idolatry" (3:4–5). Paul calls greed idolatry because he wants to alert us to this specific kind of greed and the danger it poses. Our attitude toward money can become the worship of a false god.

Jesus concludes at the end of the parable of the dishonest steward, "No servant can serve two masters. He will either hate one and love the other, or be devoted to one and despise the other. You cannot serve God and mammon" (Lk 16:13). *Mammon* means money and the stuff money can buy. It comes from the same root word for "to trust or rely upon." Idolatrous greed trusts "stuff" instead of God.

Notice Jesus does not say that we can't serve God and the devil, an obvious impossibility. He says that we can't serve God and our stuff. Our greatest temptation away from worship of God is our stuff. We see this all the time in our culture. People can't worship God, because they're preoccupied with their stuff: their houses, cars, kids' schools, kids' sports programs. Social media replaces daily prayer; Sundays are spent worshiping at the altar of the NFL or any number of other entertainments.

Paul reminds us, "Indeed, religion with contentment is a great gain. For we brought nothing into the world, just as we shall not be able to take anything out of it" (1 Tm 6:6–7). Contentment makes sense when people of faith trust God. We enter and leave this world with empty hands.

By identifying the greed that is idolatry, Paul was following rabbinic tradition, which considered greed a grave sin and one to be avoided (although by Jesus' time religious leaders had largely disregarded their own teaching). In reviving this teaching against greed and preaching contentment, Paul is establishing one of the building blocks for the new Christian community, whose worship will be pure. Free of idolatry, the Church will grow.

# Principle 3: The Church Grows through Cheerful Giving

Paul spends chapters 8 and 9 of his Second Letter to the Corinthians focused on giving and generosity. In the eighth chapter, he praises the Church in Macedonia and their exemplary charity in providing for the Church in Jerusalem. He congratulates them not only for *giving* but also for their *enthusiasm* for giving. Paul praises the Macedonians for their excessive altruism. In turn, he challenges and encourages the Corinthians to similar charity.

Next, he offers a basic fact about giving that powerfully promotes generosity. He writes, "Consider this: whoever sows sparingly will also reap sparingly, and whoever sows bountifully will also reap bountifully" (9:6). Paul uses an image from farming that's simply obvious: you reap what you sow. Then he connects his point to giving, and indeed, living: "Each must do as already determined, without sadness or compulsion, for God loves a cheerful giver" (9:7).

Giving sometimes feels like loss. We may not want to give to God, or anyone else. Giving can be an emotional struggle. Paul works to dispel our resistance by teaching us to reframe our notion of giving. Don't think of giving as *diminishing* your resources but *investing* them. It is sowing seed. The farmer cheerfully sows seeds because he knows that eventually he will have a harvest, produce, product, and even more seed to plant for the future. If we can grow to see giving in the same way as does the farmer, then we'll discover cheerful, not reluctant, giving.

Giving is to be undertaken confidently and cheerfully, already understanding the rewards. Christ followers give with glad hearts because they know that you can't *out-give God*. As Paul goes on to say, "God is able to make every grace abundant for you, so that in all things, always having all you need, you may have an abundance for every good work" (9:8). Giving opens us up to receiving: getting from God what we need to do good.

Paul continues, "The one who supplies seed to the sower and bread for food will supply and multiply your seed and increase the harvest of your righteousness. You are being enriched in every way for all generosity, which through us produces thanksgiving to God" (9:10–11). Here Paul tells the Corinthians that they are actually being enriched for the purpose of generosity. God gives to us not simply so we can enjoy the gift itself, but also so we can learn to be generous and give to others. This just makes sense.

> **Tom:** Sometimes I come home with treats—pizza, chocolates, or donuts—and entrust it all to just one of my seven kids, with a purpose. The gift is not intended for just *one* of them. I want the chosen one to be generous with the rest. That's what Paul is talking about. He concludes, "Through the evidence of this service, you are glorifying God for your obedient confession of the gospel of Christ" (9:13).

*Giving* actually glorifies God, and it attracts others to the Church. Over and over again in scripture, we find this same simple point: *giving gladly* serves as a key ingredient to the Church's growth from its very beginning.

This principle holds true not only for the early Church but for the Church in our generation as well. Growing parishes have growing budgets. When parishioners gladly give more, the parish can do more! And cheerfulness is attractive. People don't want to be part of a needy community that nags for money. But they're easily attracted to a parish that sees money as a tool for serving and fueling its mission.

When people are giving, they're growing as disciples in most other ways too. Givers are more likely to serve, get into a small group, go on mission trips, and invite their unchurched friends to come out to discover who we are and what we offer. Simply stated, the Church grows through *cheerful* giving.

# Principle 4: The Church Grows through Generous Giving

Even a casual reading of the Acts of the Apostles and the Epistles of Paul reveals that the first Christians were generous because the Church promoted *generosity* as a basic value and expression of discipleship. Generosity and giving are praised over and over again. Acts states in chapter 2, and then repeats in chapter 4, that believers shared "all things" in common—that's generosity. "All who believed were together and had all things in common; they would sell their property and possessions and divide them among all according to each one's need" (2:44–45).

The early disciples voluntarily surrendered their possessions to the Church. They would even sell their property, which in Israel was considered a birthright tied to their sense of identity, and give the proceeds to the community. While it seems likely that some of these early Christians were people of substantial wealth, many likely were not. Their giving didn't come from any kind of financial margin. Many were making their offering from the very money needed for basic subsistence.

Acts 10 tells us about a Roman soldier named Cornelius. God arranges a meeting between Cornelius and Peter to demonstrate to Peter that Jesus died for everyone—Jews and Gentiles alike. Now, among the Christians, even Roman soldiers are welcomed and included in the new covenant of grace. Cornelius himself explains an angelic vision in which he is told: "Your prayer has been heard and your almsgiving remembered before God" (10:31). God could have picked any number of Romans to help Peter recognize the universality of the Gospel, but he chose Cornelius because of his almsgiving.

Throughout his letters, Paul praises the generosity of some of the churches of the ancient world. He thanks the Philippians for their multiple gifts in support of his ministry. As mentioned above, in Paul's Second Letter to the Corinthians he praises the Macedonian churches for their giving and generosity at length: "We want you to know, brothers, of the grace of God that has been given to the churches of Macedonia . . . the abundance of their joy . . . overflowed in a wealth of generosity . . . beyond their means" (8:1–3). Paul therefore encourages the Corinthians to grow as disciples in the manner of the Macedonians: "Now as you excel in every respect, in faith, discourse, knowledge, all earnestness, and in the love we have for you, may you excel in this gracious act also" (8:7).

Generosity needs to be encouraged; it will not happen by accident. We don't drift into giving. People will drift into debt. People will drift into greed, but not into giving. Encouraging generosity helps the Church excel.

**Tom:** As a side note, this passage is included in the Lectionary, but unfortunately, the verses used fail to convey the true meaning of the text and entirely miss what it has to say about money. In fact, one Saturday night after Mass in which this was read, Michael and I were discussing the passage. We noted that we could not make sense of the reading, so we looked it up for context and discovered, to our surprise, that it was *all about money*.

# Principle 5: The Church Grows through Equal Sacrifice *Not* Equal Gifts

The Acts of the Apostles tells us that the Church in Antioch grew under the leadership of Paul and Barnabas. As it grew, a group of prophets came from Jerusalem. They warned the Church in Antioch that a famine was coming and, as a result, the Church in Judea would require relief. Even though the famine had not yet taken place, the Church in Antioch gave to this future need. Acts tells us that "the disciples determined that, according to ability, each should send relief to the brothers who lived in Judea" (11:29). They determined that each would give based on *ability* to give.

The reality is that there is a great temptation to think of sacrifice in terms of dollars and not *ability*. This temptation must steadfastly be resisted, however convenient or attractive it appears. If we want to raise givers *and* make disciples, attempts to think of giving in a dollar amount is never the right approach. The "$8 a week" idea flies in the face of the actual biblical standard of equal sacrifice, *not* equal gifts. Disciples give according to ability, not according to a fixed dollar amount.

# Principle 6: The Church Grows by Promoting Planned Giving

Paul twice tells the Corinthians that he is coming to visit them and will be asking them to contribute to the Church in Jerusalem. He notes that the Church in Galatia has already done this. He writes, "On the first day of the week each of you should set aside and save whatever one can afford, so that collections will not be going on when I come. And when I arrive, I shall send those whom you have approved with letters of recommendation to take your gracious gift to Jerusalem" (1 Cor 16:2–3). This planned giving has a twofold advantage. First, it takes the pressure off the Corinthians to give just *because* Paul is present. Deciding in advance to give would eliminate giving out of guilt. Paul doesn't want the collection going on when he is in town, because they might not give freely. Second, people would potentially be able to give more. They could save what they could afford to set aside, rather than just giving whatever money they happened to have at hand. Paul also wants representatives of the Church in Corinth to go to Jerusalem, so they can see the impact their gift is having on the Church there.

Paul repeats this message to the Corinthians in his second letter to them. He tells them that he knows they *intend* to give, but he is writing in advance, so that they can be *prepared* to support the Church. "I thought it necessary to encourage the brothers to go on ahead of you and arrange in advance your promised gift, so in this way it might be ready as a bountiful gift and not as an exaction" (9:5). Paul makes the point that planned giving is not only more helpful and effective, but it also feels right.

Giving spontaneously or even as an afterthought is certainly charity, but because human nature is often opposed to giving, our spontaneous giving is especially susceptible to greed. We have come to call chucking spare change into the passing collection basket "tipping God" for its effortless, even thoughtless attitude. Giving out of guilt is also giving to God, but not with the heart he is looking for. Neither approach does anything to build the Church, since nothing is ever different as a result.

In our preaching and teaching, we never guilt people into giving and we don't nag. Neither do we "nickel and dime" parishioners with constant requests for special collections and intrusive fundraisers. And we only pass the basket *once* during Mass.

But once a year, and only once a year, we devote a whole weekend to a stewardship commitment to our parish, *for the coming year*. We touch on the parish finances, but we don't dwell on our needs. Instead we focus on parishioners' need to give, *in their place of worship, as an act of worship*. Then we leave time at the offertory for everyone to fill out a pledge card and make a specific commitment to give in the coming year. If they prefer they can take the card home and bring it back the following week. We call this Stewardship Sunday, and most everyone at Nativity considers it one of the best weekends of the year. The details don't matter. What is important is that we invite parishioners to plan their giving.

And here's our point, as they planned their giving, the Church in Corinth grew, just as Paul knew it would. Planned giving moves us beyond guilt or greed and allows us to consider our commitment in a thoughtful and prayerful way. It allows room for the Holy Spirit to touch and change our hearts and bring us to a more generous response. In turn, planned giving will always lead to greater giving and more mature givers. As a result, the Church grows.

# Principle 7: The Church Grows When Members Adopt New Lifestyles

As you read through the Acts of the Apostles, it's easy to see that the movement of the early Church affected people economically. Converts to the faith would sometimes sacrifice their own livelihoods for the sake of their faith. At the same time, nonbelievers would oppose the early Christians because the movement threatened their own economic interests.

Converts, whose lifestyles had been in conflict with the Christian way of life, recognized their need to repent as part of their conversion, then as now. In Ephesus, this included practitioners of the magical arts and sorcery, which was a commonplace and thriving retail operation in the city at the time. In Acts we read, "A large number of those who had practiced magic collected their books and burned them in public. They calculated their value and found it to be fifty thousand silver pieces" (19:19). As a sign of their conversion and resolve never to return to their former ways of life, these magicians publicly burned their sorcery books, which were antithetical to Christianity. The book burning was a radical act of faith, and one that would have astounded onlookers. Their conversion came at a cost: fifty thousand silver pieces was a fortune. Besides, they were renouncing lucrative careers. But they willingly surrendered their financial health and future for their newfound faith.

On the flip side, we see that when some people had their economic interests threatened by the Church and the advancement of the Gospel, rather than repent, they responded with hostility. One example of this is also found in Acts 19. As Christianity was growing in Ephesus, a silversmith named Demetrius became alarmed. Ephesus housed a famous temple, to the goddess Artemis, one of the most widely venerated deities of ancient Greece. The temple was a popular destination for pilgrims and tourists and, as such, generated its own industry, an important part of the Ephesians' economy. In particular, silversmiths in the town profited through the manufacture of silver shrines of the goddess, essentially temple souvenirs.

Demetrius foresaw the threat this new faith posed to his prosperity as well as to others in his profession. He anticipated that the spread of Christianity could diminish or even destroy his industry. Followers of Jesus no longer worshiped Artemis and, therefore, no longer purchased pagan statuary. So he rallied the other silversmiths to oppose Paul and the Christians, arousing such a ruckus that he almost succeeded in starting a riot.

Another example is found earlier, in Acts 16, which relates an episode concerning Paul's time in Philippi. There, a slave girl became interested in Paul's preaching and followed him everywhere for days. That sounds like a win, but it was actually a complication.

The girl suffered possession by an evil spirit, which gave her the ability to tell fortunes. Her owners successfully marketed her mysterious talent and evidently turned a profit. Acts somewhat humorously recounts how this girl began to annoy Paul, who came to recognize she was probably possessed. So, he exorcised her of the spirit. But in the process, she lost her fortune-telling ability. As a consequence, her owners lost their star attraction and the income she provided—a great deal of money, scripture tells us. When they realized what has transpired, they responded badly, as might be expected, and created a great deal of trouble for Paul.

Whenever and wherever the Gospel is preached, lives are being changed; and in the process, lifestyles are changed too. The Church grows through these changes. If we are making disciples of Jesus Christ, then we will be challenging the people in our pews to consider how they make their money and how they spend it.

Seeing our work as a reflection of our faith means a reevaluation of our work habits or professional standards and conduct. If we come to understand the money in our hands not as *our money* but as *God's money*, it will certainly change the way we pursue money. In turn, spending on pastimes and pleasures inconsistent with our Christian living such as pornography, gambling, overindulgence in alcohol and other drugs, will need to be laid aside. And in just this way, the Church grows.

# Principle 8: The Church Grows When It Provides Materially for Its Leaders

In the ninth chapter of his First Letter to the Corinthians, Paul is answering objections to his authority as an apostle. There had been some kind of attack on his credibility, which seems to have called into question his material support from the Church in Corinth. He writes, "My defense against those who would pass judgment on me is this. Do we not have the right to eat and drink?" (1 Cor 9:3–4). Paul argues that he and his companions, as leaders of the Church, should be compensated for their ministry. He goes on, "Who ever serves as a soldier at his own expense? Who plants a vineyard without eating its produce? Or who shepherds a flock without using some of the milk from the flock?" (1 Cor 9:7). In every sector of society, in any line of work, employees deserve just compensation for their honest efforts. The same should be true in the Church. Those who devote their professional lives to the Church deserve material compensation.

Paul continues, "If we have sown spiritual seed for you, is it a great thing that we reap a material harvest from you?" (1 Cor 9:11). The spiritual life is of higher value than the material realm. So, it makes sense for those who serve people's spiritual lives to be compensated with material gifts (which are of lesser value). For Paul there is an obvious correlation: "Do you not know that those who perform the temple services eat [what] belongs to the temple, and those who minister at the altar share in the sacrificial offerings? In the same way, the Lord ordered that those who preach the gospel should live by the gospel" (1 Cor 9:13–14). We know from elsewhere in scripture that Paul was able to support himself as a tentmaker and often did not seek recompense from the Church. But here he is arguing for a principle, not compensation for himself.

In his First Letter to Timothy, Paul also considers the importance of giving to support other ministers, writing bluntly, "Presbyters who preside well deserve double honor, especially those who toil in preaching and teaching . . . 'A worker deserves his pay'" (5:17–18).

Elsewhere, Paul tells the Romans that he is going to Jerusalem to bring a contribution to the Church leaders in Jerusalem, from the Church in Macedonia: "For if the Gentiles have come to share in their spiritual blessings, they ought also to serve them in material blessings" (Rom 15:27). Paul notes that this gift he is bringing to Jerusalem was a voluntary gift from the Macedonians, but at the same time, he considers it as something they ought to have done regardless. It was probably Paul who prompted the offering, and he mentions this gift to the Romans to encourage them to do the same.

In part, for Paul, this is an issue of justice. And in equal part, it is a matter of common sense. Sharing material gifts with the Church is not an act of generosity, but something they ought to do. You have an obligation to leave a tip for good service at a restaurant, and if someone has blessed you spiritually, you should provide them with material blessings.

Another motivation for Paul to encourage the Macedonians and Romans to support the Church in Jerusalem was to unite the Jewish and Gentile Christians. The financial gift would form a bond between the givers (Gentile Christians) and the receivers (the Jewish Christian leaders). In the same way, we have found that a parish fosters unity when members support the staff financially. This is a critical lesson for today more than ever. Most people, in our experience, have no idea of what it costs to run a parish, and many Catholics are still not accustomed to having professional staff members in ministerial leadership who are not ordained or members of a religious congregation of sisters or brothers. These professionals need to be compensated fairly for their work.

**Tom:** After all the years I have been here in the parish, I still get parishioners who will ask, "So, what do you do for a living?" Even after all this time, I must admit, I am still annoyed by the question.

We need to pay staff in part because it is a matter of justice. Their jobs are real jobs in which they really work. And they deserve compensation for their work. As a Church community, we have no business talking about justice to the larger culture if we're not promoting it for our own employees. But it is also a simple, obvious fact that we will not be able to attract and maintain the talented people we need moving forward unless and until we are offering fair and reasonable compensation. This is obviously of increasing importance as parishes rely on lay staff more and more.

**Father Michael:** During our annual stewardship weekend, I always highlight our staff. I remind the parishioners that staff members have families and homes and financial needs, just as they do. I make the case that they deserve a living wage, so they can actually afford to live in the community they serve. As pastor, I take responsibility for staff salaries, and I have a distinct advantage in this task. Since as a diocesan priest my salary is fixed, I, like Paul, am not asking for myself.

On our stewardship weekend, we ask all staff to be present because we want to show our congregation the people whose salaries are paid by their giving. We tell our team that it is in their best interest to be present, so we can continue to fund their work in the future.

If you belong to a parish, consider this: If everyone gave as you did, would the church be able to pay the people who are serving you and your family a just wage? It's an important question. Supporting staff is often lost in our consideration of giving. If someone blesses you spiritually, bless them materially.

**Tom:** Likewise, if someone blesses you *materially*, bless them *spiritually*. This is a principle that can apply to everyone but especially to those of us who work on parish staff. We can be praying for the donors in our parish. Part of our weekly staff holy hour, therefore, is devoted to prayerful support for our donors.

As our parish has grown, our funding for staff salaries has also grown. And we believe strongly that these two things always go together.

# Principle 9: The Church Grows through Funding Mission Outreach

The early Christians cared for one another both locally and globally. As we discussed above, Paul encouraged Christians throughout the world to take care of the Christians in Jerusalem who were especially lacking in material wealth. In Acts 11, as well, we read that the disciples decided to help the Christians in Judea, who were, at that time, suffering from a famine. Paul tells the Corinthians that he visited various communities and encouraged this offering (see 1 Corinthians 16:1).

Like the early Christians, we must lead our congregations to be concerned about meeting the needs of Christians around the world. As churches in first-world countries, we should intentionally fund international Christian ministries, especially those in less developed countries.

Beyond just passing the basket for a second collection, look for opportunities in your parish to promote giving to other Christian ministries. Help your parishioners get excited about the impact their giving and the ministries it funds have on the broad mission of the Church. If you paint the right vision, then giving will beget *more giving*. And it will not detract from but actually build enthusiasm for the parish offertory.

In the process, as you are a blessing for other churches and ministries, your parish will be blessed. You will experience church growth through this kind of giving.

# Principle 10: The Church Grows by Teaching the Rich How to Be Rich

Paul writes in his First Letter to Timothy, "Tell the rich in the present age not to be proud and not to rely on so uncertain a thing as wealth but rather on God, who richly provides us with all things for our enjoyment" (6:17). Paul tells Timothy to instruct the rich, which begs the questions, Who is rich? And what makes someone rich? While we cannot be forgetful of the poor among us, for those ministering in parishes in developed nations, many of the people we serve *are* rich. They enjoy comforts and conveniences unknown to most people in the world, today and throughout history. Teaching the rich how to be rich is first of all about helping them recognize their wealth.

When people have more than enough, they can easily be blinded to the reality that it is God who is the source of their very ability to make and manage it. Affluence can numb us to the blessings and advantage of a favorable economy; abundance can blind us to a nation of laws that respects private property and the buying and selling of goods. Teaching the rich how to be rich is about helping them appreciate the favor they enjoy.

And notice that Paul doesn't tell Timothy to teach the rich to despise their money or distance themselves from it, though they should take no pride in it. Yet, neither is money to be relied on in the manner in which we should trust God and God alone, to whom all wealth ultimately belongs. This point is an especially important one. Sometimes in churchworld we inadvertently or deliberately try to make people feel guilty for having money. Essentially, this is on par with making them feel guilty for the gifts God has given them. And that's a fruitless and unbiblical exercise that works against God, disrespects his people, and does nothing to help the parish. People do not grow in generosity out of guilt, nor does guilt motivate people to become more fully devoted followers of Jesus Christ.

God doesn't want the rich to feel guilty. He loves the rich; he died for rich and poor alike. God doesn't want the rich to feel guilty, but to feel grateful and give expression to their gratitude in their generosity. Paul instructs Timothy about the dangers of wealth: "Those who want to be rich are falling into temptation and into a trap and into many foolish and harmful desires, which plunge them into ruin and destruction" (6:9). Then Paul delivers one of the most famous—as in famously misquoted—lines of all time: "For the love of money is the root of all evils" (6:10).

Pink Floyd simply got it wrong, and many others before and after them have too. It is not money that is the root of all evils, but the love of it. It comes down to an issue of the heart. Wealth is not the problem, but greed in the human heart is. A consuming desire for wealth inevitably introduces harmful habits and unhelpful pursuits that can be even more destructive.

This is an especially important message for us Americans enmeshed in the rampant consumerism of our culture. Every day we are reminded of what we don't have and tempted by what we didn't even know we wanted, confusing more stuff or wealth with *more happiness*. Paul recognizes this confusion about wealth: "Some people in their desire for it have strayed from the faith and have pierced themselves with many pains" (6:10). In a cost-benefit analysis, it isn't worth choosing money over God. It's not good for believers' health—their *heart* health. This might be one of the most important lessons to teach the rich how to be rich.

But here is the most important lesson of all: "Tell them to do good, to be rich in good works, to be generous, ready to share, thus accumulating as treasure a good foundation for the future, so as to win the life that is true life" (6:18–19). When the rich are rich in charity, they grow. And in the process, the Church grows too.

Giving and Church growth go together:

- inviting God into our finances
- rooting out greed from our hearts
- giving cheerfully and generously in a deliberate and planned way

- calling forth equal sacrifice from all our parishioners
- promoting planned giving
- inviting giving at a level that actually impacts lifestyle
- inviting giving that supports and sustains our spiritual leaders *and* helps those in need
- inviting giving that spiritually assists the wealthy

All these will help the Church grow.

Of course, to make all or any of that happen, you've got to raise givers.

# Part III

# ASKING FOR MONEY IN OUR PARISH

# 7

# RAISING GIVERS
## *9 STEPS WE TAKE*

Wealth is not about having a lot of money; it's about having a lot of options.

—Chris Rock

**Father Michael:** Early on in my time here, a parishioner asked to meet with me about making a donation. Naturally, I was interested in sitting down with her to discuss a possible gift. In preparation, I looked up her giving history only to discover she had none. There was no record of any donations or even a single gift to the parish, although she was a founding member, never-miss-a-Sunday kind of Catholic. She was also someone of obvious means.

Elizabeth was the kind of person whose outsized personality could fill a room and easily dominate any conversation, which is exactly what happened at our meeting. She lost no time in coming right to her point: "I don't give to this parish because Nativity doesn't need my money."

I immediately moved to convince her that nothing could be further from the truth. She quickly cut me off: "Nativity doesn't need my money, and you know it. You may *want* my money, but that's not the same thing, is it?" This back-and-forth went on until it became clear I would not change her mind, so I just conceded the argument.

But what was this meeting about? Elizabeth wanted to commission a statue for the church and had already selected an artist and a prominent location near the altar. Sounds great, right? Not exactly. No kidding, what she was proposing was a substantial marble sculpture of St. Elizabeth, cousin of Mary and mother of John, but it just so happened that the artist's rendering she had in hand bore a striking resemblance to herself. She wanted her name carved into the base as a permanent memorial of her generosity.

We passed on the statue, much to Elizabeth's everlasting annoyance. And we never did learn what became of her sizable estate. Needless to say, the parish didn't receive a cent.

That visit would have provided us with a very helpful lesson, had we had enough experience to recognize it. She very succinctly summed up two sides of the same coin when it comes to the attitude of many parish givers:

1. The Church just *wants* my money, but they don't *need* it.
2. I'll give in exchange for something I want—which, of course, isn't really giving but is a consumer transaction.

Since that meeting with Elizabeth, we've developed nine crucial steps toward establishing a culture of generosity and raising givers. None of these steps is incredibly difficult. Neither will they prove to be rocket science. But they continue to produce results.

## Step 1: Begin in Prayer

Raising givers and moving people to give to the Church is ultimately a spiritual exercise. And since it is a spiritual exercise, we cannot move people to give only by our own power. We need the Holy Spirit to touch and change people's hearts. This is true of any spiritual step but especially when it comes to the issue of money and finances. As Rick Warren says, there is a very sensitive nerve that runs from the heart to the purse.

Without regular prayer, we cannot hope to increase the level of giving in our churches in a way that is consistent with making disciples of Jesus Christ. You don't need prayer to manipulate people out of money. But it is indispensable if you want to change their hearts and move them to changing their lives through giving. We learned to make prayer a part of every effort to raise the giving level of our church.

Ask your eucharistic adoration or Rosary teams to make it a special intention. Remember parish giving and givers at daily Mass and, from time to time, in the Universal Prayer on Sundays. Form a prayer group to lift up your stewardship efforts on a regular basis. Create special worship events that include the whole parish.

A few years ago, we launched a capital campaign to build a brand-new sanctuary to accommodate our growth (the church is now completed, and we write about the experience in a later chapter). We kicked off the campaign with forty hours of prayer and eucharistic adoration. This was forty consecutive hours from 6:00 a.m. one day to 10:00 p.m. the following day. We invited the whole parish to come and pray for the upcoming campaign and thousands did. We came to believe that this first step was the critical step to the campaign's success.

## Step 2: Lead with Your Own Giving

If you are reading this book, it is probably because you're a leader in your church and you want it to succeed financially. In fact, you want to see your ministry and vision fully funded. For that to happen, something else has to happen first: *you* have to give.

In order for the finances in your parish to grow, you must go first when it comes to giving. And your giving must be generous and whole-hearted. In the third chapter of Malachi, we read how God reestablished the challenge of the tithe for the people of Israel. But before he challenged the people, he chastised and challenged their leaders: "A son honors his father, and a servant fears his master; if, then, I am a father, where is the honor due to me? And if I am a master, where is the fear due to me? So says the LORD of hosts to you, O priests, who disdain my name. But you ask, 'How have we disdained your name?'" (Mal 1:6). How was it that the priests who were supposed to teach and lead the people to honor God through giving were utterly and completely failing to do so themselves? How did they go so wrong? "By offering defiled food on my altar!" (1:7).

The Law commanded giving God the best—that which cost the most. When it came to blood sacrifices, that meant healthy animals, valuable livestock. However, the priests were selecting defiled animals, the ones they didn't really want for themselves because they were basically worthless. It was a sacrifice, *sort of.* It just didn't cost them anything. To dispel any doubt, the passage goes on to detail the exact problem with their sacrifices: "When you offer a blind animal for sacrifice, is there no wrong in that? When you offer a lame or sick animal, is there no wrong in that? Present it to your governor! Will he be pleased with you—or show you favor?" (1:8).

Most people wouldn't think of inviting their boss over for dinner and serving leftovers. You'd never dream of giving a damaged gift to someone you want to honor or impress. And yet, that is exactly what these leaders were doing before God. Moreover, on top of this effortless, worthless sacrifice, they sought the favor of the Lord, only adding insult to injury. And we do the same thing when overlooking or ignoring our own giving.

God says to these leaders in response, "Oh, that one of you would just shut the temple gates to keep you from kindling fire on my altar in vain! I take no pleasure in you . . . and I will not accept any offering from your hands! . . . You say, 'See what a burden this is!' and you exasperate me, says the LORD of hosts" (1:10, 13). The exchange is ultimately futile and comes down to a problem of the heart. The priests look at their offering as a burden. They are not cheerful givers. They see giving only as something to be gotten over with, a game to be played at, but one that is ultimately meaningless to them.

If we are to lead people in our pews to become more generous givers, we need to examine our own perspectives and consider our own motives in giving. And that may well mean a change of heart. We must develop hearts that embrace giving as a privilege of our leadership. We found that, unless and until we did this in very deliberate ways, there was no change in the parishioners' giving either.

> **Tom:** Each year before our stewardship weekend, Michael and I take our commitment cards and pray over them for a week or so. After we make our commitments, we place our cards on the altar, where we will eventually collect the commitment cards of the whole parish. As Michael preaches his stewardship message challenging the parish to commit to give for the coming year, our cards bear silent testimony to our own commitment. We never ask anyone to do anything we aren't willing to do first.

> **Father Michael:** So, too, before our most recent capital campaign, Tom and I were the first to make commitments. We had already decided that we would be approaching this campaign in a nontraditional way, which we explain in a later chapter. Before we took this approach to the parish, we challenged each other. Our own commitments launched a very successful campaign. It has been amazing to see how God has stretched our faith as we fulfilled, and eventually surpassed, our commitments.

We're convinced leaders have to give first. But the challenge actually goes deeper than that. We're also convinced that leaders need to give *most*.

*What?* Yes, you've got to give *the most*. You cannot allow any member of your parish to surpass your *level of giving*. Others, obviously, will give more in terms of their dollar amount, because they have greater financial resources. But the generosity and sacrificial giving of your parish will never rise above the generosity and sacrificial giving of your leaders.

# Step 3: Teach People What God Says about Money

Over the course of both our Catholic educations, there were lots of appeals for money. But the subject of what God says about giving never came up.

**Father Michael:** This was also the case when it came to our parish. Early in my tenure as pastor, I gave a stewardship homily in which I mentioned tithing just once and in passing. After Mass, a woman approached me shaking her finger in my direction. She proceeded to chide me angrily, "I never want to hear *that* word in this church again. That's a Protestant word, and it has no place here." And for a long time, I never used the word, even though it is God's word. My parish remained ignorant of what God has to say about money. And I had nobody to blame but myself.

As parish leaders, we need to take the responsibility for teaching people God's lessons on how to handle money.

**Tom:** And the principle way we teach people about God's view of money is by *preaching* it clearly and consistently. Michael preaches in "message series," exploring a single topic over a series of weeks. On several occasions in the past, he has actually offered whole message series on money. But more often, he just preaches about it as often as it comes up in the Lectionary, which is *a lot*. Then, we make sure the message is reflected in our other forms of communication, such as our small-group discussion materials, our electronic daily devotional, and even our children's Liturgy of the Word.

Sometimes people in our pews are so confused and overwhelmed in their finances that they are in no position to give anything to anyone. That's why we offer money classes. Currently, we use Dave Ramsey's Financial Peace University. Members of our parish can sign up for the class and learn solid financial practices that will help them succeed with managing their money. This includes forming habits such as budgeting, saving, eliminating debt, investing, and, of course, giving. As people learn and follow biblical financial strategies, they will be ready for the next step. Our financial office also offers one-on-one financial counsel for those who might benefit from personal assistance.

Clear, consistent teaching and preaching that is *not* yoked to any kind of ask is indispensable. When it comes to sharing our message about money, we make sure to emphasize that it is not what we want *from you*, but what God wants *for you*. Over the course of seasons and years, graciously and respectfully teaching people about money can change hearts and minds.

## Step 4: Ask

Leadership is simple. It's about getting people to move from one place to another. And more often than not, that simply comes down to *asking* them to move.

People do not naturally move or spontaneously change on their own. We tend to like the status quo. This resistance is true for any proposed movement, more so in a spiritual one, especially when it comes to giving. Most people will never increase their giving—or, for that matter, even start giving—without being asked to do so. It can happen, but waiting for people to decide on their own that they want to give, or give more, is not a reliably successful strategy.

Asking is a good strategy for success. And *how* we ask for money matters greatly.

People do not give to neediness. Not really—not in a sustained, long-term committed way. They may respond to an urgent or unprecedented need, such as a natural disaster, but most people grow cynical with persistent, chronic neediness. And any suggestion of financial mismanagement or lack of planning can turn that cynicism into anger.

People do not give to neediness. They give to a *vision*. When you ask people to give to the church, paint a vision for what their giving will accomplish. Paint a vision in two major ways.

First, paint a vision of what giving accomplishes in *their lives*. Teach potential givers that when they start giving to God, they'll begin experiencing God's hand in their finances. Giving actually invites him in, and making giving a priority can take faith to a whole new level. In other words, teach them about all the personal benefits of giving to God. Let them know about the difference giving has made in your own life.

Second, paint a vision of the difference their giving can accomplish for *the lives of others*. Share stories of lives changing and the impact your parish has had on your community. We've produced videos featuring parishioners giving personal testimony of what giving has meant to them. On other occasions, we've read testimonial letters.

A new practice we've developed is something we are calling "giving moments." From time to time, just before we take up the offering, we play a video highlighting some aspect of our parish programs or services: kids' programs, youth ministry, pastoral care. Oftentimes people, even established givers, simply don't appreciate or know where their money goes. These attractive videos teach them what their giving makes possible.

In whatever way you choose to do it, the point is to offer a positive vision of how the money invested in the parish will change people's lives, starting with the lives of the givers themselves. Ask people to support a grander purpose and a greater good, and keep reminding them of that vision by telling stories. Everyone wants their lives to matter, and if we can show that giving to our church makes a difference, our parishioners will give.

Aside from vision, it is important to identify the time or season of the year when you are going to ask for money. Our stewardship weekend is scheduled for the Sunday before Thanksgiving (which is the fourth Thursday in November here in the United States). We have found this timing to be helpful for a few reasons. People are usually in a good mood with the holiday approaching. Also, the overall culture helps promote a spirit of giving in that season. Finally, it is close enough to the end of the year that people can begin planning for the year ahead, but not so close to Christmas that our ask gets swallowed up by the holidays.

> **Father Michael:** On Stewardship Sunday, we only ask for *money.* This is a practice we strongly encourage. When we first started celebrating stewardship weekend, we would also invite people to think about gifts of "time and talent." Our stewardship cards even had a place where you could indicate that you were interested in volunteering. This is a common approach. It's also a mistake because it weakens the ask for money and waters down the message. We know that many, if not most, people are so very reluctant to give their money away that they'll take any excuse to avoid it. Each year, when we tabulated the responses that we received on those pledge cards, there were always many more commitments to *volunteering* than to *giving.* And most of those commitments were never kept. On the other hand, we've discovered that if we get people to give, it's easy to get them to serve. They're invested.

> **Tom:** Remember our elderly accountant Frank? He volunteered his time a couple of days a week as the parish accountant. Funny thing was, he didn't support the parish financially. At all. During our very first stewardship campaign, I approached Frank about making a commitment to give not only because we needed his support but also because we needed his good example. He had his answer ready: "The time I give to this parish is worth $20,000 a year. That's my gift." Given the financial constraints we were under at the time, I would rather have had the cash.

We say that "time is time" and "money is money." God wants us to give *both.* Both are required to grow as disciples of Jesus Christ. But at Nativity we designate other times of the year when we ask for people to volunteer their time to serve. Stewardship weekend is all about financial giving.

For a long time we only had one annual ask—on Stewardship Sunday. During our capital campaign, however, we obviously had to host a separate Commitment Weekend. Another ask that has developed over the last few years funds mission projects we are promoting. We find this works especially well in Advent. We have raised money to build schools, dig wells, and invest in micro economies. One Christmas we established a school lunch program in a village in Haiti, and the next we provided school supplies, uniforms, and books for a village in Nigeria. These and other mission projects were easy asks to make, extremely well received, festive, and fun. They were also successful. Giving on mission weekend has grown robustly year after year, becoming a revered holiday tradition.

One other ask comes with the annual diocesan appeal, which is a practice currently found nearly everywhere in this country. Making this ask can be a bit more challenging, even in the best of times. Following the post-2018 abuse crisis, however, such fundraising may present a higher hurdle. We have found that the heavy-handed tactics sometimes suggested are not always the best strategy for raising up long-term givers. Much more helpful is to emphasize the good and great work that such appeals are making possible.

> **Tom:** All these asks should come from the pastor in the pulpit, but others in the parish can lend their voice too. For example, in the weeks leading up to Stewardship Sunday, I make a brief announcement before the first reading, letting the congregation know Stewardship Sunday is coming up. Since I usually do them, these announcements have come to be branded as "Tomilies." We also use this time to hand out our commitment cards.

Finally, when it comes to asking for money, we need to be aware of donor fatigue. One of the reasons people think that the Church is always asking for money is because many times we *are* always asking for money.

# Step 5: Put Rungs on the Ladder

Imagine a ladder with all the lower rungs removed. It wouldn't be very useful for climbing. Sometimes churchworld can seem like that. The churchpeople are on the top of the ladder. With the lower rungs removed, the unchurched are left with no chance of climbing up. We churchpeople can make it mighty difficult for the unchurched to come to church, even when they want to.

This has been a problem for churchworld from the very beginning. At the Council of Jerusalem, the apostles debated if Gentiles had to become Jewish in order to become Christ followers. The apostle James ruled, "It is my judgment, therefore, that we ought to stop troubling the Gentiles who turn to God" (Acts 15:19).

When it comes to financial support for their parish, many people have no history of giving and little interest. For some, just showing up is their contribution. Then, we proceed to inundate them with fundraisers, appeals, and special collections that nickel and dime them while raising only a pittance of what the Church needs to fund its mission.

How do we get people on the path of giving as God calls them to give, and then help them grow as givers?

As noted, the biblical standard is the tithe, but as we've also seen, God doesn't just want the tithe. He wants us to acknowledge his ownership of everything and to diligently embrace our role as stewards of what we have and hold. And while we actively and enthusiastically encourage members of our church to tithe (and even go beyond the tithe), besides the two of us, probably very few do. That's okay.

We need to put rungs on the ladder. Our rungs are the following, from bottom to top:

- planned giving
- priority giving
- percentage giving
- progressive giving

Rather than just confuse or annoy people with a message about giving 10 percent, we instead challenge them to take these steps, climbing the rungs on the ladder.

If you're just throwing change into the basket on Sunday as an after-thought or out of guilt, we challenge you to plan your gifts instead. Each year we invite every parish household to make a commitment to their *plan for giving* in the coming year.

Next, the challenge is to establish giving to the offertory as *a priority* in the parishioners' budgets. And eventually, the challenge is to make it *the* priority in their budgets—to make sure their gifts to the church come first over any other expenses.

*Percentage giving* comes next, and it brings the key change in think-ing. We like to say that it's not about the *10* in the *10 percent*—it's about the *percent*. Percentage giving is the major cultural shift to get people moving in the right direction.

And, believe it or not, as people become committed percentage givers, the *"progressive"* part takes care of itself. Once you get the other rungs in place, this one happens automatically. People want to continue giving and to give more than they ever have.

## Step 6: Set Them Up for Success

At a stewardship conference we attended a while back, the keynote speaker asked if there was anyone present who had more than $100 in their wal-let. Out of an audience of several hundred, one man stood up. Fifty dol-lars? Two more stood up. How about a check—was anyone carrying their checkbook with them? Not one.

The fact that people rely on cash and checks less and less seems almost entirely lost on churchworld. We expect people to preorder envelopes, fill them out before Mass, remember to bring them to church, and then donate their cash or checks in the collection baskets. This is the way we collected money in the Church fifty or sixty years ago. The rest of the world has moved on.

There is an argument to be made that the offertory is an established and important part of the liturgy, which includes the offering of money. It should remain so, as a significant symbol of the gift we are giving as we come before the Lord. But inevitably, it will become increasingly symbolic. The actual collection of funds will become electronic.

Establishing a convenient, accessible way for your members to make recurring donations, through electronic funds transfer, credit cards, or even texting, is an essential step in setting your parishioners up for success when it comes to giving. That it happens *electronically* means it happens *automatically*, which in turn means it actually happens. Despite people's very best intentions to give, it is all too easy to forget the offering, to leave the giving envelope at home or in the car. And, of course, there is always time off and time away, holidays and vacation, kids' sporting events, and the occasional snowstorm. Many surveys find that the average Catholic who self-describes as attending church "weekly" is only attending *your church* about thirty-five weeks of the year. That's seventeen weeks a year when they're simply not present and may make no offering at all.

Electronic funds transfer (EFT) can become part of a parishioner's plan to give and ensure that they actually fulfill that plan. Meanwhile, the more of your *parish giving* you can move to *electronic giving*, the more solid and sustainable your parish finances will be. So, in setting parishioners up for success, you're setting your parish up for success at the same time.

If you don't currently offer EFT at your parish, there are many third-party providers who can assist you in this service. Then, consistently promote it to your parishioners. We emphasize the value and importance of automatic giving every year on our stewardship weekend. We preach that it is the easiest and the most helpful way to give. On our stewardship cards, we have a place for parishioners to mark that they are interested in signing up for automatic giving, and then we take care of the process from there.

In addition to EFT, parishes should also provide parishioners the choice of giving with credit or debit cards. This should be an option on your website, too, where people can give anytime they think of it, such as when they are paying their bills. Giving on your parish's mobile app or through texting are especially convenient options.

Electronic giving isn't the next generation of giving; it's the new normal. And getting out of the business of collecting, bagging, storing, counting, and depositing cash and checks is most certainly a very good development. EFT and online credit card giving now represent nearly 60 percent of all of Nativity's offertory transactions and are the fastest-growing types of giving at our parish.

# Step 7: Celebrate Giving / Celebrate Movement

Truett Cathy, the founder of Chick-fil-A, liked to ask, "What is the telltale sign that someone needs encouragement?" The answer: "They're breathing." Everyone needs encouragement to do good. As scripture instructs us, "We must consider how to rouse one another to love and good deeds" (Heb 10:24).

In a culture that constantly tells us that the key to happiness is more stuff—especially more *money*—we need to remind people that giving, not spending, is the wisest use of their money. We must invite them to give and encourage them to keep giving.

And the very best, most effective way to do that is to celebrate giving. This is especially the case when people begin to give, even more so if they are new to the parish, or new to church giving. As churchpeople, we take our offering as an unquestioned responsibility. Unchurched people are not of that view. Their first-time gift is an expression of newfound trust in you and your church that should be celebrated.

Think about building into your accounting process some way to identify first-time givers, givers who increase their offering, and one-time gifts.

And then acknowledge this movement. If you send givers an end-of-year financial statement, why not include a hand-written note of thanks from the parish or the pastor?

Our "giving moments" videos are all about celebrating giving. Each video is a positive presentation that feels good and expresses our gratitude.

Celebrate giving, and celebrate positive movements in giving, because what gets celebrated gets repeated.

# Step 8: Ruthlessly Eliminate Competing Systems

**Father Michael:** When I first became pastor at Nativity, an older pastor whom I respected greatly reached out to me. My respect for him was largely based on his financial prowess when it came to the administration of his church. He had taken a financially struggling parish and built it into a fundraising powerhouse. He gave me a lot of wisdom and insight that, as a first-time pastor, I very much needed. But one piece of advice stood out—because, as I would later learn, it was wrong. He told me, "Mike, you've got to pass the basket as often as you can get away with it, because every time you do, you *will* make money." He always had a second collection at every weekend Mass, and sometimes even a third.

**Tom:** Awhile back, a friend counted five separate appeals for money during his visit to a neighboring parish. There was the first collection, announced by the pastor with an urgent request for support in view of budget woes, as well as a second collection accompanied by a visiting religious who spoke about her appeal. There was an Advent Giving Tree in the sanctuary, the youth group was selling cookies in the lobby, and the Knights of Columbus had a Christmas tree sale on the parking lot. Plus, in the parish bulletin even more fundraising appeals could be found. All those asks can hurt each other as well as the long-term efforts of the parish to raise money.

**Father Michael:** While we are on the topic: I don't allow other people to use my pulpit for their purposes. I understand that others want to leverage the crowd we've gathered at our church to financially support their organizations. But that is not our responsibility, however worthy their effort, however noble their need. We have the most important mission and message in the world, and all our efforts on the weekend must focus on our mission—ours not theirs. That may seem coldhearted, but we can't serve more than one master.

Once we became convinced of the hardwired connection between discipleship and giving, some other things also became clear. As we've already discussed, we simply could not hold on to methods that coerce or trick people out of money, nor was guilt a helpful tool in teaching disciples how to give. And distractions (such as fundraisers or second collections) create competing systems to our givers.

Author and psychologist Henry Cloud says, "Losers go for fruit." Think about it. Anyone can shake fruit out of a fruit tree. It takes much more effort and time to plant, cultivate, and prune a fruit-bearing tree. Losers go for the fruit, because it's quick and easy and bears immediate results.

So many traditional parish strategies for giving rely on short-term efforts that raise cash but actually discourage discipleship. In fact, they are often transparently shortsighted and self-serving. Ultimately, this can be a losing strategy if it creates confusion about your mission, leads to donor fatigue and cynicism, and diminishes long-term results. Ruthlessly eliminating competing systems requires discipline and a long view on giving. It also takes a bit of courage.

Over the past few years we have eliminated all second collections. Along with their giving envelopes, parishioners receive special envelopes supporting the monthly collection request by the United States Conference of Catholic Bishops. If they choose to support any particular collection, they simply return the corresponding envelope in the offertory collection. But we do not pass the basket twice. Historically, in our parish the second collection only yielded between 2 percent and 5 percent of the first (depending on the collection), so we make up for any shortfall out of our operating budget.

Passing the basket once also better serves the liturgy as a powerful sign, a stronger symbol, of our worship offering, not diminished by repeated requests.

In our recently completed church we deliberately omitted the old-fashioned "poor box" at the entrance. Instead we reserve a percentage of our budget for the poor and our missions' efforts (a percentage, by the way, far in excess of what the poor box ever took in).

Eliminating competing systems also means getting rid of fundraisers. Some fundraisers are expressions of ethnic or community identity and as such can be maintained. Others are part of an old model that aims at tricking people out of their money. Maybe you can't afford to cancel all your current appeals and sales in the same year. So, start with the big, ugly fundraiser, the one nobody wants to do, the one that's the most draining on resources and raises the least revenue. When the dust settles, the complaints die down, and the parish has recovered from the financial hit of some lost revenue, go after the next one. Eventually these pruning exercises will bear amazing fruit, far in excess of your fundraisers. That's why you must show them no mercy.

## Step 9: Persevere

In our various travels and conferences since publishing *Rebuilt* in 2013, perhaps the most frequently asked question we get is, "How long?" "How long will it take to rebuild? Sixty days? Six months? Six years?" Well, of course every place is different, but the short answer is, "A *long* time." However long it takes, it is going to take a long time. Changing a church culture takes time, and changing people's giving habits is changing the most entrenched part of your culture. It will take a long time.

Long obedience in the same direction is needed to create a culture of giving. We like to think of preaching and teaching on money as launching rockets at a wall. People build up walls around their hearts, walls that block them from following God. This is true in many areas of life, but money walls are some of the thickest. Our job is to keep firing the truth of God's word into those walls until they crumble and fall. This takes perseverance.

If year after year you:

- pray for giving to increase,
- lead with your own giving,
- focus on what God's word teaches us about money,
- ask people to give to a vision for your parish,
- make giving easy and accessible,
- eliminate competing systems,
- gratefully celebrate and thank your donors . . . , and
- persevere . . .

then you will see substantial movement in the financial health of your parish.

# 8

# ENGAGING HIGH-CAPACITY GIVERS

## *9 GREAT IDEAS WE STOLE*

---

**F. Scott Fitzgerald:** The rich are different from you and me.
**Ernest Hemingway:** Yes, they have more money.

Warning: Do *not* skip this chapter!

This is a chapter you may be tempted to overlook because you think you don't have any high-capacity givers in your parish. You live in a blue-collar community, or a rural setting with lots of people of modest means. You're a church of struggling immigrants or retirees on fixed incomes. So perhaps this does not seem to apply to you. Here's the fact of the matter: no matter your socioeconomic context, you have people who are your top donors or who could be. Wherever you live, there are obviously people who have a higher income or more money than the rest of the community and, if cultivated, can have a great impact on your budget and in the life of your parish.

**Father Michael:** Our second capital campaign came as a consequence of our initial growth as a parish. Our church had a dysfunctional, undersized parking lot, virtually no lobby or gathering space, and absolutely no fellowship space. When Mass was over, our facility firmly communicated, "You need to leave now." We definitely wanted to change that, so we decided to build onto the front of our building.

We were looking at a project initially estimated at $1.5 million. It actually ended up costing more (a lot more), but even so, that number was a big one for us at the time. We were wisely advised that the place to get started was with a quiet phase, reaching out to potential donors. These asks could help us craft our message and, if successful, build our confidence to launch a parish-wide campaign. We identified three such opportunities.

Helen was one of our most dependable donors on the higher end of giving, and a fan of what we were doing in the parish. Not all of our senior citizens were enchanted with us and the direction in which we were headed. Many of them would stand in strong opposition to this building project. Helen, however, had caught the spirit of what we were working toward, and I was sure she would support us. I was right—partly.

When I sat down with her, I explained the plan and then asked her point blank for a specific gift. I said, "Helen, I need $50,000 from you to get this project started." Not one to mince words, she replied: "I was going to give you $100,000, but if fifty is all you need, here you go." She pulled out her checkbook, wrote a check for the full amount on the spot, then got up and left. I sat there dazed. I didn't know if I had just made $50,000 or lost it. Worse still, Helen never again gave us another gift or offering of any kind.

Will, like Helen, was one of our top givers, but not exactly a fan. His giving to the parish sprung from a sense of long-term commitment; it was *not* an expression of support. He had, in fact, from time to time used his giving as a wedge to make certain demands. I had permitted him to do so because, well, he was a bully, and I was intimidated by him, and because the parish needed his money. I allowed myself to be coerced, a shameful reaction I now deeply regret.

When I sat down with him to share our vision for the new construction, I didn't get very far. He had come armed with a list of every grievance and perceived offense he had ever supposedly suffered at my hands. His list was extensive and, in various places, entirely fabricated or lavishly embellished. If I had recognized that he was so disaffected with everything we were doing, I would have spared myself this debasement. He knew he had a golden opportunity to tell me off, and he took advantage of it. We did, eventually, get a lead gift from him, but only after we were subjected to even more complaints and demands. Reluctantly, I agreed to give him naming rights for the project. That's another regrettable coercion I would never again allow, as you'll read about in the next chapter.

Mel was not actually one of our top donors, but all available information and evidence strongly suggested he easily could be. Besides, he seemed completely integrated into parish life and quite content with what we were doing. He gladly agreed to sit down with me and seemed genuinely interested in the project—the operative word there being "seemed." When I had completed my presentation, he politely began to riddle it with questions that graciously picked it apart. At first, I didn't realize what was happening and went along with this delicate, uncomfortable dance. But eventually it became clear he would not be supporting us, and he was building his case for why not. Basically, it came down to his lack of interest in financially supporting the parish. It was another disappointing and humiliating encounter. Eventually, Mel and his wife withdrew their modest annual contributions and left the parish.

When it came to Helen, I had underestimated her giving potential and, in the process, insulted her. It was a miscommunication. Will was a disaffected parishioner and used the opportunity of our campaign to embarrass me and insist on his demands in exchange for his contributions. It was extortion. Mel was an especially sad story. He wasn't really with us, but all things being equal, he had seemed fine. The capital campaign changed the equation and forced him to choose a side. It was a declaration.

The fact of the matter was, once again, we had no idea what we were doing. Today, we would not repeat any of those unwise approaches with potentially high-capacity givers. To move forward we had to ask and find answers to some serious questions.

In preparing for this book, we had lunch with a friend, Matt, who is an effective fundraiser for his very successful nonprofit. He especially does a great job cultivating high-capacity donors. We asked, "What's your secret?" Matt responded, "Engage them."

While this suggestion is simple enough, it raises other questions. First of all, is it right to invest in people just because they're wealthy? It doesn't seem Christ-like.

In the New Testament, we read, "Show no partiality as you adhere to the faith in our glorious Lord Jesus Christ. For if a man with gold rings on his fingers and in fine clothes comes into your assembly, and a poor person in shabby clothes also comes in, and you pay attention to the one wearing the fine clothes and say, 'Sit here, please,' while you say to the poor one, 'Stand there,' or 'Sit at my feet,' have you not made distinctions among yourselves and become judges with evil designs?" (Jas 2:1–4). James sets up a hypothetical situation in which a wealthy person and a poor man walk into a Christian assembly. The man of wealth is given preferential treatment, while the poor guy is treated, well, poorly. In other words, greater value is accorded to the person of greater wealth while the poor are marginalized at best. He seems to be arguing that we should *not* show any partiality to people with means or give them extra attention. But that's not his point. He's not talking about fundraising. Treating the rich and poor with equal dignity and respect is what James is teaching.

Also, we should note that the scene James paints is in regard to someone coming to *worship* within a Christian *assembly*, where all believers, of whatever station of life, stand together equally as children of God. Certainly, we need to be aware of the temptation to treat people of means *better* than we treat other members of our parish. But that danger should not keep us from engaging the wealthy for giving purposes.

Of course, beyond the question of dignity, there's still the fairness question. It doesn't seem fair to give more time to people simply because they have greater wealth. Many people, especially churchpeople, argue that we should be completely egalitarian in approaching parishioners for donations. We ought to ignore income when we decide how we spend our time. Otherwise, we are not being fair.

Fairness ended in the Garden of Eden. Nowhere does Jesus teach us we need to distribute our time equally among parishioners. In fact, his life modeled just the opposite. He spent considerably more time with the apostles than he did with the crowds or the other disciples. And even among the apostles, he made more of an investment in Peter, James, and John than he did among the other nine.

You might be thinking, "Yes, but those were the apostles who were going to lead the Church." That's true, but in the gospels, we also see that Jesus gave greater access to people who supported his ministry. In Luke we read, "Afterward he journeyed from one town and village to another, preaching and proclaiming the good news of the kingdom of God. Accompanying him were the Twelve . . . and many others who provided for them out of their resources" (8:1, 3). Luke notes that Jesus gave special access to "many others." Why did he do that? Because they paid the bills. They made his ministry possible, so he afforded them more of his time and attention. There was nothing untoward about that. They weren't "buying access" to Jesus. They were supporting his work, and that was the basis of a special relationship. Was Jesus playing favorites? Actually, he was providing us with an example.

Likewise, Paul had people of means who funded his ministry. In Acts 16, Lydia provides hospitality for the apostle, giving him a place to stay and meeting his basic needs. She was likely in a strong position to support him because the text notes she was a dealer in "purple cloth," in other words a high-end retailer. In return she obviously enjoys a favored position in the ranks of his disciples.

So, if it was good enough for Jesus and good enough for Paul, it's probably good enough for us. There are people in your church whom God has gifted with the ability to make and invest, save and spend, money. They know how money works and take full advantage of the opportunities they encounter. If we ignore those gifts, we are failing as leaders.

God does not distribute gifts equally among his children. We see this clearly in the parable of the talents, where one steward receives five talents, another two, and another one. Why doesn't God distribute gifts more evenly? We don't know, but scripture and our experience affirm this reality.

We are all challenged to grow in generosity and called to honor God through our money and possessions. But some people have received a greater capacity to give because they have been given the ability to build wealth. There are those who can make a larger impact for the kingdom through their finances because that is how God has blessed them.

Investing in relationships in order to help the whole Body of Christ move forward financially is not falling into the sin that James is describing. The wealthy can be a special blessing to God's people if they are engaged and invited to use their resources to build God's kingdom.

Perhaps we don't engage people of means because we fear that their support creates a debt. We'll owe them, and they'll have control over us. We prefer not to be obligated to anyone for anything. This is a legitimate concern born out in many of our experiences at Nativity. Whatever anyone gives to the Church should be a gift. That means it comes with no strings attached. It shouldn't be about buying access, manipulating decisions, or demanding outcomes, but supporting the work of the ministry. It is true there are people out there who will try to work you; they are to be avoided. Don't allow yourself to become manipulated like we did with our friend Will.

**Tom:** We are not saying that people never give with poor intentions or mixed motives. It has happened in our church on a regular basis. Major givers have threatened to withhold their contributions if we (really Michael) made decisions they didn't like. In those cases, we (really Michael) went ahead and made the decisions they didn't like anyway, and at the cost of their support. It hurts, but personal integrity offers no other choice. You never should be beholden to anyone except God. However, you can follow God and engage the wealthy in your parish. They are not mutually exclusive. Our bet is that if you constantly make the connection between discipleship and giving, you won't have major donors who use their money for manipulation or control.

Most of the wealthy people we have gotten to know in our parish give because they have been blessed by God. They don't give to buy special privileges. There isn't all that much we can offer them anyway when it comes to favors. Actually, our major donors are among the kindest, humblest people of integrity that we've met.

So the question is, how do you do it? Here are our ten ideas for engaging high-capacity givers.

# Idea 1: Get to Know the Attributes of Givers

Leaders in giving all share certain attributes that we need to recognize and cultivate.

**Tom:** When we began our most recent capital campaign, we were advised that we would need at least one gift of $1 million in order to make our goal. I joked, "I'll write the check today. It won't clear, but I can write the check." I would have loved to support the project at that level more than anything. I just didn't have that kind of money (I still don't).

The first attribute of a lead giver: they must have the *ability to give* at a level above the norm. *Desire to give* isn't enough, however deep the desire. Potential lead donors must have *capacity*. Capacity, however, is a matter of not just dollars and cents but *spirit*. Some people have the *financial* capital but lack the second attribute of a lead giver, *spiritual* capital. And if we push them to give before they have the spiritual capital, we can stunt their growth so that they never become great givers.

Second, a high-capacity giver must value generosity and giving. God has blessed many people with wealth who do not understand that they have been blessed *to be a blessing*. We learned that unless and until a person of means realizes that giving is a good use of money, they will not be big supporters of our work.

A third attribute of high-capacity givers is that they buy into the vision and mission of our church. There are hundreds of thousands of nonprofits doing good and great work in the arts and sciences, health care, higher education, addiction recovery, poverty reduction, urban development, and the list goes on and on. They're all competing for the charitable dollars available in our communities, and nearly all are worthy of support. People with a capacity to give are targeted constantly and solicited ceaselessly. And that can mean they're overcommitted before they ever even consider giving to your parish.

**Father Michael:** In most of the conversations I've had with high-capacity givers, the first thing they uniformly say when sitting down together is, "Father, I love our parish and support you're work, but I am all tapped out."

Wealthy people with a heart for giving will give *somewhere*. They'll give proportionately to their understanding and belief in the vision and mission of a nonprofit or charity. This is why we need to invest in our donors by casting a vision, articulating our mission, and telling our story. And we need to keep preaching and teaching the vision because it can fade and people forget.

Of course, if the people of means in your parish do not hold these attributes, they can always develop them. With your help, anybody can grow into a great giver.

# Idea 2: Get to Know Who Your Givers and Potential Givers Are

Basically, we have three options as church leaders when it comes to our givers.

We can ride the wave of those who are already giving, making it our goal to get as much money out of them as often as possible, for as long as possible, with as little effort as necessary. We can guilt, ambush, manipulate, flatter, or whatever works to keep givers giving.

A second option is that we can simply ignore the giving issue altogether and, in the process, ignore individuals who have the potential to be lead donors. This is actually the approach of far too many parishes.

There is a third option: we can *get to know* our potential leaders and learn to engage them, which might take humility and creativity.

**Father Michael:** When first coming to the parish, I was approached by a gentleman who, I later learned, was someone of tremendous means. He asked to see me, and when we met, he said simply, "Father, I have the ability to help this parish in a significant way; please use me." He went on to explain that he'd made the same offer to my predecessor on several occasions, to no avail. "What happened?" I wondered. He answered, "I think it was pride, coupled with an utter lack of imagination."

Admittedly, this might seem incredibly obvious, but if you don't know who the high-capacity potential givers are in your parish, or what is on their minds and in their hearts, then you will not engage them. When it comes to this information, we approach it from very different perspectives.

**Father Michael:** I actually don't want to know what people give, at least not in detail. As pastor, I don't want their giving to color my view of them.

**Tom:** I do. I want to know in detail on a weekly basis. And I want to have those numbers readily available for referencing, anytime I interact with donors. I know all of the top one hundred donors in our parish by name, and I'm in regular communication with them. I make sure Michael knows who the top fifty donors are and that he is reaching out to them, at least from time to time.

Along with knowing who the current top givers to our parish are, we learned we had to develop a sense of who our *potential* givers could be: people who currently don't give but could. Quite honestly, we're not exactly firing on all cylinders when it comes to this one, and we know we can do better. But at least we understand its importance and the path forward.

For instance, there are people in your parish who *know* people. They know the influencers, the leaders, the movers and shakers in your community. Network with them. Ask for their help in identifying people of means.

**Tom:** Sometimes I will invite these folks to just stand with me in the lobby on Sunday mornings and discreetly point out parishioners whom I don't yet know and who have giving potential.

Another way to identify high-capacity potential givers is by looking ahead to the next generation of givers. There are members of your parish who are not yet able to give at a level higher than the norm, but they are on that track. While still early in their careers, get to know who they are, and help introduce your parish into their evolving philanthropy.

# Idea 3: Build the Relationship

As we noted above, *people* give to *people*. Relationships, therefore, are key. Like everyone else in the pews, givers already have a relationship with you if you are the pastor or a prominent staff member. The people in the pews know you, or at least they think they do. Our job is to get to know them.

> **Tom:** In addition to meeting people, I also spend my time before and after weekend Masses looking to connect with the high-capacity givers we already know to check in and catch up. But sitting down to break bread together can be a powerful way to jumpstart or advance a relationship. Of course, you have to decide what works best for you and your schedule. Breakfast meetings are going to be short and therefore focused. Dinner is a bigger commitment of time and can be more of an expense. We prefer lunch.

Over the past few years we've developed the practice of lunch meetings, two or even three times a week, which one or both of us attend. Usually these take place at local restaurants—nothing fancy, but places where we can sit down and talk. Other times we have carryout at the office.

Usually, the lunch meetings are set up based on names that come to our attention because of their giving. A candidate can be anyone who starts giving, increases giving, or makes a significant stand-alone gift. Other invitations come at the recommendations of parishioners, suggesting someone we should get to know. We are clear upfront that we have no agenda. We found this to be extremely important because people assume our invitation means we want something from them. Of course, we do want to encourage their giving, but not as a part of an initial meeting. Knowing that, they relax.

At lunch the conversation is unrehearsed and easygoing, usually starting with family history: where people grew up and went to school. We always ask when they came to the parish and what brought them to us.

Feedback, comments, even criticism are all welcome, although in such a setting they are always softer than might otherwise be the case.

If we're in a restaurant when the bill comes, we of course take care of it. We invited them and we want to say thank you. They're our guests.

We keep notes on these meetings, including upcoming events in the lives of their families and challenges they're facing. This might sound coldly calculating, but it is actually a strategic attempt to grow leaders for the parish. People lead with many kinds of gifts, and as we've pointed out, funding our mission is crucial. So, we create a record of our interactions because these potential high-capacity givers are important to us. Birthdays, anniversaries, special requests, and prayer requests can easily be acknowledged or become the subject of future conversations. And our remembering can mean a lot.

Not long ago, news stories uncovered major problems at a prominent corporation. From our lunches, we knew that one of our largest donors serves on that corporate board. And from the news accounts, we could easily imagine that he was going through a difficult time. We took the occasion to reach out to him and let him know of our concern. He texted back his thoughts on the situation and thanked us for the prayers. It was another way to build our relationship and tend to the spiritual needs of a person who may become a key parish leader.

One couple shared with us that their daughter-in-law was struggling with infertility. We followed up by sending along a St. Elizabeth's medal and prayer (she is the patron saint of mothers, and, just for the record, the daughter-in-law was soon expecting). Another friend talked excitedly about his daughter's upcoming wedding. We reached out to him in the days leading up to the ceremony and helped with his speech for the reception.

Another family was planning their daughter's wedding while the mom was dealing with a serious health challenge. We stayed in touch with them through the period of preparation with assurances of support. In the end, the wedding went off beautifully, the mom is doing great, and our relationship is stronger than ever.

It's about building the relationship, and it actually costs you nothing.

# Idea 4: Give Them Access

**Tom:** Wait, didn't we say earlier that people who give shouldn't influence a parish leader's decisions or determine outcomes? Yes, but by offering your givers access, we mean *relational* access. In our lunches, Michael shares stories about his childhood, where he grew up, how he came to Nativity, what he likes to eat, what he does to relax (well, actually he doesn't relax, but that's a different book). People are generally very interested in the pastor's personal history. They want to get to know the person who is standing in the pulpit every week teaching them how to live their lives. This gives them access to his life in a way that others do not have. For the record, key ministry leaders and council members also enjoy the same access.

Another way to give someone access is to invite them to stop by the sacristy or drop into the pastor's office after Mass for a quick visit, just to touch base. Obviously, you can always give people access by sharing your phone number and email. Of course, that means nothing if all your contact information is already on your bulletin. But if you're selective about who you share it with, it will mean something.

Although we have not taken this step ourselves, many pastors are very successful at organizing trips or leading pilgrimages. Not everyone is cut out for that, but it can prove to be a bonding experience for sure.

# Idea 5: Give Them Insider Information

Information is a kind of currency, especially when it comes to insider information. Sharing it with high-capacity givers could be a real value to them. Before announcing to the parish upcoming or special events, tell high-capacity donors first. If there is a problem on the horizon, give them a heads-up. With donors we're also very transparent about expenses and the parish budget, which might not be helpful to share with the parish at large.

A monthly email with updates on what is going on can be a very efficient way to keep your donors in the loop (and *feeling* as though they're in the loop).

Simply stated, communication is easy, inexpensive, and terrifically effective in engaging high-capacity donors.

# Idea 6: Ask for Input / Seek Their Advice

Everybody likes to be asked for input. And most everybody is more than happy to share their opinions. Same for our donors. We ask for their input and advice on issues we're facing, challenges we're anticipating, and opportunities we see developing. This just makes sense, since often people who have done well financially built their wealth with solid judgment and wise instincts.

As scripture says, "Precious treasure and oil are in the house of the wise" (Prv 21:20). Wealth and wisdom don't *always* go together, but they *often* do. You can learn a great deal of leadership skills and life lessons by seeking out the advice of successful people in your community. And then listening to it thoughtfully.

# Idea 7: Thank Them

**Tom:** When we first started getting serious about stewardship by reaching out to donors, I will admit I was uncomfortable. Consequently, I approached those early conversations in a shy and sheepish kind of way. Over time, I have gradually gained the confidence I need to succeed. And what helped me grow, more than anything else, was coming to understand the power of gratitude.

Beginning a conversation about giving by thanking someone for their previous gifts not only feels good but also sets the right tone. A quick word of thanks in a passing exchange works well too. And a telephone call can be very much appreciated in response to a significant or year-end gift. Best of all, a good old-fashioned hand-written note from the pastor does not go unnoticed. In fact, it can be an extremely powerful way to express that we think what they're doing is important. We've actually gotten thank-you notes for our thank-you notes.

Any way you do it, you can never overdo it. Recently, we reached out to once again thank a donor who had given a transformative gift to our capital campaign. Going into the exchange, it felt unnecessary. But as we expressed again how much his gift meant to us, we could immediately see how much our expression of gratitude meant to him.

# Idea 8: Pray for Them

Whenever we interact with donors, we add a pledge of prayer, and we ask how we can pray for them. It's not just feeding them a line. We really want to pray for them. And we do. Here's a tip: as soon as you promise to pray for someone, do it. Do it immediately, and you've kept your basic promise. But obviously, you can do more.

**Tom:** As part of my daily quiet time, I have developed the habit of remembering and raising up our donors in prayer, keeping in mind the needs and intentions they've shared with us. Each week our staff gathers for a holy hour, and sometimes a portion of this time—or even the whole of it—is given over to prayer of intercession for our donors.

Pray for your donors, and it is definitely okay to let them know you're praying for them. Whenever we sit down with donors, the last question we ask is, "How can we be praying for you?"

**Father Michael:** "Pray for them" can sound like banal church speak. And yet we know that, when actually relied on, the promise of prayer is very powerful. I remember meeting with a couple who said that they were praying for their son who had walked away from the church. I emailed them the next day just to let them know I had joined them in prayer for the young man. They were thrilled and humbled that I remembered him.

**Tom:** Another time, I had an impulse to pray for a generous donor and texted him to let him know. Quite honestly, it sounded strange even to me, but I did it anyway. I was glad I did because later that day he texted me back heartfelt thanks. His daughter had just been through a traumatic experience hours before, and he very much appreciated the thought and prayerful support. We have found that as relationships grow with our donors, it's easy to see the Holy Spirit moving among us.

# Idea 9: Keep Your Motives Pure

Maybe one of the reasons we don't always develop our relationships with the wealthy is because we're afraid of doing it for the wrong reasons. Or we've seen others operating out of mixed motives, perhaps taking advantage of parishioners for personal gain, favors, or advantages.

We've all known pastors (and parish staff) who have inadvertently, or quite intentionally, developed a culture in which people give to *them*, instead of to the *parish*. Expensive meals, golf outings, ski vacations, club memberships, cash at Christmas—the list goes on.

One of the struggles wealthy people face is that they don't know who likes them for *who they are* and who likes them for *what they've got*. No one wants to feel used. And of course we don't want to be the kind of people who use others. As parish leaders, we want something *for* people, not just *from* them. However, we have to acknowledge that, as church workers, we are just as fallen as everyone else. If we are not careful, we will come to use people. Instead of seeing people Jesus died for, we will see only dollar signs.

But we should not let the danger of mixed motives keep us from developing high-impact givers. In anything we do, we can go astray when it comes to our motives. This is why scripture says, "With all vigilance guard your heart" (Prv 4:23). If we stay heart-healthy and ask God to keep us single-hearted, we can avoid the trap of using people for their money.

We keep our motives pure when we seek always to honor and respect our donors, and when we remember that our role is not to worry about outcomes or results, but to build *trust*. We can invest the time and build the relationship. We can make the ask. But we can't make anyone give. God has to move people's hearts.

In *A Spirituality of Fundraising*, Henri Nouwen paints a picture of the right kind of heart in describing his relationship with a wealthy banker and his family. He writes, "The money was real, but it was not the most impressive part of our relationship. We all had resources: mine were spiritual and theirs were material. What was impressive was that we all wanted to work for the kingdom, to build a community of love, to let something happen that was greater than we were individually. My banker friend helped me see that we must minister to the rich from our own place of wealth—the spiritual wealth we have inherited as brothers and sisters of Jesus." The wealthy are different than we are, and they're also very much the same.

As F. Scott Fitzgerald reputedly said, "the rich *are* different." Wealth brings both distinct privileges and unique challenges that the rest of us don't face. People of means don't have to worry about being able to pay bills on time or finding money for retirement savings. Probably, they do not have many unmet material needs or unfulfilled desires. All of which sounds good, but with more money comes more responsibilities. It can complicate relationships and bring expectations and demands others don't have.

Some people of means can struggle with guilt over what they have. A sense of shame can cause them to downplay their affluence, keeping privileges and perks low-key. They can even become apologetic about it all. At the same time, perhaps, they are inundated, even overwhelmed, by requests for giving. We can always remind them that they don't have to feel guilty about their money, because it isn't even *theirs*. It's God's money, which he has entrusted to them for good and great work. We can walk with people as they grow in their giving, inviting them to understand that their resources can also be a spiritual gift.

Ultimately, we are hoping to set up a win-win-win situation. High-capacity donors win when they use their money to build God's kingdom, using some of their temporary treasure to build an eternal one. Parishioners benefit from a financially healthy parish. And meanwhile, we grow as leaders to better help build the kingdom with our particular gifts.

**Tom:** F. Scott Fitzgerald was right, but so was Ernest Hemingway. People are people no matter how much money they have. They still need a Savior. They still need Jesus to save them from their sins.

During our most recent construction, one of our high-capacity givers, also named Tom, wrote us a note after sitting down with us over lunch. At that meeting we introduced him to Sue, who runs our operations and managed the construction of our new sanctuary. She gave our guest a tour of the construction site, explaining the project and answering questions. After the tour, and the time spent with Sue, he wrote to Michael:

> Dear Father Michael:
> I want to share an impression I have formed in the last eighteen months since we first came to Nativity. I spend my days looking for investments in growth companies for our clients. The most important factor we absolutely

demand before making an investment is confidence in the management team and the people involved in the company. We want a leader who is more concerned about the success of the company and its mission than personal glories and who is surrounded by very talented people. When I think about Nativity under your leadership and the bright dedicated people you have surrounded yourself with (Tom, Ed, Sue, Brian, and so many others), you have followed the blueprint for what we have found to be very successful enterprises. Pam and I are very pleased to be invested in the future of your mission. If you were a public stock, we would buy shares!

When it comes to high-capacity givers, they're looking for solid investments. We have to show them that is exactly what our parish is. We're definitely not begging; we're not even fundraising. We're inviting their *investment*.

- Know the attributes of givers.
- Get to know who your givers are or could be.
- Build the relationship.
- Give them access and insider information.
- Seek their input and advice.
- Thank them.
- Pray for them.
- Keep your motives pure.

And you will be building a solid core of high-capacity givers in your parish.

# 9

# WHAT WE LEARNED FROM OUR CAPITAL CAMPAIGN

## *14 RECOMMENDATIONS WE ENDORSE*

Teresa [of Avila], without the grace of God, is a poor woman; with the grace of God, a force; with the grace of God and a lot of money, a power.

—St. John of the Cross

A capital campaign is an intense, stand-alone effort on the part of a church or nonprofit organization to raise a specific, usually significant, amount of money within a designated period of time. In most cases, it funds a building project or a capital improvement that will advance the mission of the organization. A capital campaign can be incredibly important in the life of the organization. In fact, it can make or break it.

A parish we know, in another part of the country, provided us with a powerful cautionary tale not very long ago. They undertook a capital campaign to build a new building. The proposal called for the construction of a parish hall, which the church didn't have. The parish had plenty of land to build on, and the design was a handsome one that was generally well received. Also, it is important to note that the parish enjoyed the leadership of a solid and sensible pastor, who had been in place long enough to earn most everyone's trust. Oh, and the economy was strong and the parish affluent. So how did they do? Knocked it out of the ballpark, right? Wrong.

From the beginning, the project was wrapped in mystery, which became ongoing and powerful grist for the gossip mill. When plans were finally introduced to the parish at large, the rollout came in a ham-handed way that tended to create more confusion than clarity. At no point was anyone ever asked for their input, and there was no opportunity to raise questions or express concerns. So questions and concerns multiplied. Neither did it help that the associate pastor and the faith formation director were not on the same page as the pastor. Behind the scenes, they were sowing discord and doubt about the project. That was a big problem that the pastor unwisely ignored.

When the parish-wide Commitment Weekend came around, the details that make it easy for people to participate were needlessly neglected. This meant, inevitably, that a certain percentage of people just didn't bother. Meanwhile, the pastor's homily that weekend painted the campaign more as an *obligation* than an *opportunity*. The results were dismal. Nothing close to even 50 percent of the project's projected cost was pledged.

Then things got worse.

The decision was made to withhold the results of the campaign until some new plan could be formed on what to do next. To be fair to the parish leaders, they were in a tough spot. They clearly would not be raising enough money to build the proposed project, but they'd already spent a substantial amount on design development and engineering studies that were necessary even to introduce the campaign. And money was already being received for the project, as people began fulfilling their pledges.

Then the pastor did something that was entirely understandable and completely regrettable. He announced to the parish that instead of a parish hall, which was now beyond their reach, they would be renovating the church. This was a pet project that he'd been dreaming of for years, but one fraught with potential controversy given the historic character of the building.

And that was pretty much when all hell broke loose. Some people withdrew their pledges or demanded their contributions back, accusing the pastor of a bait and switch. Concerns about what, exactly, a renovation to their beloved church might mean grew hot and hysterical. And the school parents, really a community unto themselves, who had been lured into supporting the parish hall on the grounds that it would be available to their children Monday through Friday, decamped from support en masse.

One result of this response was that the parish never even collected the majority of the pledges that had been originally committed. As a result, the "renovation" turned out to be nothing more than a paint job and some new carpeting, leaving everyone disappointed. Far worse was the damage done to the credibility of the parish leadership. Not long after, the pastor gladly accepted an assignment elsewhere. And the current pastor will tell you the parish has never quite recovered, as evidenced in weekly attendance and annual giving.

In our first two campaigns we made plenty of mistakes ourselves, though through sheer luck neither of them ended as badly as the preceding story. Even now, we don't know everything about how to run a capital campaign. But as of this writing, we have recently completed a third capital campaign to build a new church with accompanying breakout and fellowship spaces. It was a big campaign for us, with a goal four times our annual income, and five times our previous campaign. There was plenty of fear and doubt as we tried to determine our way forward. We will even acknowledge a few shouting matches between the two of us (okay, more than a few).

From our current perspective, it's easy to celebrate the success of the campaign, which surpassed its lofty goal by millions of dollars. But much more important than that proud achievement is the difference the campaign made in the life of our parish. It was, in a word, transformational.

Our methods (as you might guess) differ from traditional fundraising advice and what most consultants will tell you. In fact, some fundraising professionals, both in and outside the Church, have mocked our methods. That's okay—the results speak for themselves.

Perhaps our first lesson to share is that there is not one right way to undertake a capital campaign. There are universal principles, but each capital campaign is going to look different and take shape based upon a few particular factors:

- the goal itself: *its perceived and real ability to be achieved*
- the "season" the parish finds itself in: *new or aging / growing or slowing*
- the parish leadership: *their credibility and the pastor's stability in office*
- the culture of the community: *their level of commitment and spiritual maturity*
- the type of project: *building a church, for instance, is obviously easier to raise money for than debt reduction*
- the breadth and depth of the project: *how long it will take, and whether it will impact people's personal experience of the parish*
- the marketing of the project: *transparency and clarity of communication*

No two capital campaigns are ever going to look alike. They always bring an inherent uncertainty. There is no playbook with all the right answers. Successful capital campaigns require leadership and leadership traffics in uncertainty. Just think of it as job security for the pastor.

## Our Path to a Campaign

In *Rebuilt* we tell the story of growing a healthy parish. We also grew a *bigger* parish, far in excess of what the facility we'd inherited could handle. At peak times, on Sunday mornings, we were so crowded that our building and parking lot were deeply dysfunctional. We considered every kind of incremental solution including modest additions, video venues squeezed into open spaces, and a shuttle service for off-campus parking.

These were bandages. The experience on our campus, inside and out, just didn't work, so much so that people walked away rather than try and navigate it all. We were living Yogi Berra's famous observation: "Nobody goes there anymore, it's just too crowded."

**Father Michael:** How many times have I said, to anyone who would listen, "The last thing Baltimore needs is another church"? And yet, finally, and at last, I agreed to do what I had promised myself I would never do. We would build a church and triple the size of our seating and parking capacity. As we developed our master plan, it grew in scope (they always do), and it became evident we were going to need to raise a great deal of money.

First, there was the parking, which needed to be vastly expanded. Fortunately, we had the necessary land, but with storm water management issues and other county regulations, it became a major engineering headache and a jaw-dropping expense. And, predictably, a couple of the neighbors launched a frenzied protest that was fortunately short-lived.

Then, there was the proposed building, which had to be more or less built around and integrated into our existing seventies-era church. Architecturally, that proved to be a *very* complicated project.

All of this is to say, we had to work through each of those issues before we could ever launch our campaign. And, to resolve them, we had to spend a not inconsiderable amount of money.

We had many advisors on our project (both paid and volunteer). But time and time again, at the end of the day, we ourselves had to decide which ideas we would implement, and which advice would be put aside.

Many of our counselors came from the parish and were development professionals. But none of them had any experience raising money in a church setting. Because of this we had to filter their advice, decide how it played in a parish setting, and determine how it matched with our philosophy of giving.

By the way, this does not discount the need and importance of having wise counselors. Even if you sometimes pass on their advice, the practice and the process will strengthen your campaign.

We spent long hours putting together our building plans. In retrospect, this was time well spent as we were learning how to confidently present those plans in detail to potential donors, beginning with our biggest financial supporters. However, those initial meetings were *not* about asking for money, but about inviting input. An old fundraising adage goes, "Ask me for my opinion before you ask me for my money." We cannot overstate how helpful we found this.

These meetings with our donors were important in another way, too, identifying problems or concerns the project might raise. For example, one of the questions we received, over and over again, concerned the size of the new church. People feared that the sanctuary would be so big that we would lose the intimacy of the original facility. It turned out there was an easy answer that seemed to satisfy everyone: even though there would be three times the number of seats, not one would be any farther from the altar than in the old church, given the semicircular design of the new sanctuary.

Another note on those meetings: we undertook them in a way that fit our personality and our schedules. Most were daytime meetings, which we preferred to evenings, and all were small, a size that works well for introverts like us. In other words, we established a pattern that was sustainable and a template that was easily replicated.

Next, we asked some of those initial people we met with to host parties in their homes, inviting a wider circle of their friends who could potentially provide advanced gifts when the time came. These neighborhood gatherings were more comfortable settings to engage parishioners we knew less well. Our hosts made the invitations and provided drinks and snacks, and we came prepared to make our case and field their questions. Our plans were largely well received. Where there were concerns or pushback, we incorporated those points into future presentations.

This was important groundwork for our campaign. While we were honing our message and growing in confidence, we were gaining momentum in a safe way before we ever went to the whole parish. We could meet people and talk about the project without the pressure of an "ask." It also allowed us to prepare our lead givers and supporters emotionally and mentally for what was coming. This is a necessary part of leadership that is easy to overlook: anticipating how people will think and feel about any kind of change or transition. Giving supporters *permission* to acknowledge their thoughts and own their feelings, as well as *time* to overcome their fears and concerns, is critical. It allows people an opportunity to catch up with your vision and thinking.

## Delay and Interruption

Launching a campaign takes time and money, and this one seemed to be taking a lot of both, due to the following tasks:

- master campus planning
- design development
- environmental, engineering, and traffic studies
- county approval
- diocesan approval
- meetings, meetings, and more meetings, always followed by more trips back to the drawing board

**Tom:** It began to seem as if our campaign was such a long time in coming. I was actually anxious we would lose the momentum we'd built. We had to get started. I couldn't wait to get started.

**Father Michael:** I could. To me the coming campaign looked like a huge rock rolling down a hill, and I was standing directly in its path. The campaign was definitely going to be a lot of work, if nothing else, and I was not all that anxious to get started.

Then on the very eve of the decision to finally launch our campaign, we received some new information that stopped us in our tracks.

In our master campus planning, we had investigated the potential of other properties in the area that would give us even more room to grow. There were some compelling reasons to leave our campus, but we never found any place that could have worked for us, within the territorial boundaries of our parish.

But then, just as we were preparing to go public with our campaign, a country club and golf course in our community went out of business and up for sale. The property was a beautiful one with several substantial buildings, which, it turned out, could be repurposed for our kids' and students' programs. There was plenty of existing parking, and the setting, spreading out over more than a hundred acres, would have provided a stunning backdrop for a new church building.

At first, the whole idea was so unexpected that it seemed silly even to consider, much less discuss. But in certain ways, it also began to make sense. It was estimated that if we sold our existing campus for its market value, we could buy this new property, renovate its buildings, and still have some starter funds for a new sanctuary, while also reducing the campaign goal we were currently facing. One of our very wise advisors told us, "You need to keep looking at this opportunity until God closes the door." Despite our discomfort, we knew we had to explore this option at least until it was no longer an option.

So we did. We struggled with this question for an intense period of discernment and prayer that stretched out for months. But as we continued to explore the opportunity this property presented, and we gained new information, the doors didn't look so wide open after all. Ingress and egress on the site were problematic and would probably require expensive redesign. The owners turned out to be less inclined to work with us than was initially suggested. And then there was the neighborhood association.

**Father Michael:** You never want to get in the crosshairs of a neighborhood association. I sat down with the president of the group one evening, expecting a vigorous exchange. What I got instead was an ultimatum, "Father, if you try and build your mega-church in my backyard, I'll fight you every step of the way, and so will my neighbors. And we've got the time and the money to do it." It felt as if God didn't just close the door—he slammed it in our faces.

Anyway, we had our answer. But the interlude turned out to be a blessing in several ways. Because we had waited, when we finally launched the campaign we did so in a much stronger economy. Studying the alternate property helped us grow in appreciation for our own campus and what a solid opportunity it really was, especially in terms of its location. And finally, this step back from our previous planning really did help us craft a stronger, clearer message when we did, at last, go to the parish.

**Tom:** I guess the lesson is to pay attention to *God's timing*. While we were in a rush (okay, maybe it was just me), God wanted to slow us down. If left to our own devices, we would have under-taken the campaign before we were really ready. Our patience eventually paid off.

# Naming and Launching
## the Campaign

After the alternative property fell through, the leadership team turned our sights back to raising the money to build on our current campus. The first task was to *name* the campaign. We played with many different approaches. Eventually, we landed on naming it the Vision Campaign. All along, we had said that the building project was not primarily about a building, but about the vision God had planted in our hearts to grow a healthy church of growing disciples and to help other churches do the same.

Our vision is to be a church that people who don't like church *like*. We want to be a church where the unchurched get to know their Savior in a life-changing relationship. And giving is essential to this relationship. Giving stretches our faith and helps us to make God's kingdom a priority in our lives. We took as our inspiration a verse from the prophet Habakkuk: Vision has an appointed time (see Habakkuk 2:3).

By calling it the Vision Campaign, we were emphasizing that the building would be an expression of our vision. The project would be about taking a spiritual journey together as a community. We saw the building as a bold platform for our vision to grow disciples by creating empty seats at optimal times for people who are living unconnected to Christ. And we intended the new church to be an illustration in brick and mortar of what a healthy, growing church can look like.

With our brand in place, we then set out to put together our brochures and collateral materials, both printed and digital. We intentionally wanted this campaign to look as distinctively different from previous fundraisers as its approach to fundraising would be, and that is what the new website and materials aimed at.

As with our annual stewardship commitments, both of us believed we should commit to the campaign before anyone else. We cannot quite remember just how we decided to determine our own gifts, but we landed on a particular strategy that guided the rest of our campaign.

**Tom:** Since we wanted the campaign to be a faith journey that would stretch people beyond their comfort zones, we realized we needed to do the same. Both of us committed to first identifying a gift that we could comfortably meet within our own budgets—in other words, a gift we knew *how* we would give. Then, we shared the number and prayed about it. I prayed about it with my wife, Mia. But none of our prayers were about *that* gift; it was about the gift we would make *in addition* to that gift. We then identified the gift we would make that we didn't know how we were going to give, for which we didn't know where the money was coming from. This ensured that we ourselves set off on this campaign by leaving our comfort zone behind. Interestingly, when Michael and I shared our commitments, they were exactly the same number.

In any capital campaign, the leaders must go first. They need to model the kind of giving they want repeated from the rest of the parish. If leaders are not willing to really sacrifice for a project, then there is no reason to expect the rest of the congregation to do so. Throughout scripture, we see that God works through leaders who honor this principle, and he still does so today. We cannot overestimate how important it was that we went through this process. This is not a boast. We say it because we know it was an integral part of the success of our campaign.

And here's another thing: when you, as a leader, finally commit yourself to give to God in just this way, providence moves too. All kinds of things begin happening that would not have happened otherwise.

## A Different Kind of "Ask"

**Father Michael:** At a basic level, committing to give was an incredibly liberating and empowering exercise as we prepared to ask a lot of people for a lot of money. I could go ahead and make those "asks," confident that I wasn't asking anyone to do something I hadn't already done, give anything I hadn't already given, make a sacrifice I had not made myself.

We developed a "giving chart," which is used in many campaigns, to break down the project into potential gifts that could help us meet our goal (e.g., we will need twenty gifts at $5,000, ten gifts at $10,000, and five gifts at $20,000). This helped potential donors envision themselves and their place in the campaign. It also provided an illustration of just how the impossibly big number we were looking at could, in fact, be achieved.

But we did it with a twist.

In this quiet phase of the campaign, entirely behind the scenes, we shared the giving chart. And we never, not once, asked anyone for a specific amount. Instead, we challenged people to identify the highest number they felt comfortable with, *and then* to look up to the next number. That would be the amount we were asking from them. We decided this would be the basis for the whole campaign. We would invite everyone to give in just this way.

One other thing about our campaign, and it's a big thing: as we began, we decided that there would be no "naming rights" (the practice of naming portions of the project after donors who give at significant levels). Neither would there be any kind of plaques, plates, donor-recognition trees, or legacy walls. Nobody's name was going on anything, anywhere in this project. Sure, it can make giving more attractive and "asks" easier. But we thought that it could compromise the integrity of this particular campaign. Everyone who advised us warned us strongly *against* this decision. We even wavered on it once or twice ourselves. Still, we wanted every gift to be seen as an important gift between the giver and God.

During this period, we met people with whom we'd already established a relationship. Previously we'd sought their *advice*; now we were asking for their *support*. This phase of a campaign can be incredibly difficult if you're just making cold calls. But these conversations were actually easy and enjoyable because we already had an established rapport with lead givers and we already had their buy-in. Some of the people were high-capacity givers, while others were key ministry leaders and members of various advisory councils who had been instrumental in our planning. We wanted all of them on board first.

**Tom:** We decided to host the one-on-one asks in the rectory. This allowed the conversation to be private and the environment to be controlled. It also dispensed with any awkwardness in ordering or paying that a sit-down at a restaurant might pose. Most of all, it provided potential givers with a rare opportunity to spend time in the pastor's home, moving the relationship to a different level.

We established a template for the lunches, to make them easier on ourselves: greet our guests and then offer a brief look at the house before sitting down together. The menu was planned, too, aiming at nice but not expensive or extravagant (we had tossed salad, crab cakes, mashed potatoes, fruit cups, and sparkling water or iced tea).

During lunch, we would simply catch up and connect relationally. Then, over dessert, we would transition to a discussion about the campaign. The invitation and previous communications prevented this from being a surprise. We definitely didn't want these meetings to feel like an ambush.

> **Tom:** I would introduce the topic by reminding our guests about our vision as a church, making the case that this project was an expression of our vision. Then Michael would describe the project itself, talking about the proposed building and its features. This worked well because he brought a lot of energy and enthusiasm to the presentation, being himself an armchair architect (every actual architect's nightmare client).

> **Father Michael:** And then Tom (who is pretty much tone deaf when it comes to design) would dig into the campaign details. Here, we typically fielded questions or even concerns, and this is where every discussion was different: some people were interested in the design, others the financing or construction details, still others the furnishings and finishes.

Once our presentation was complete, and we'd answered any questions, we made our pitch: "Decide where your comfort level is, and then look up."

This proved to be a great way to ask people to support the campaign. It reinforced our message that, while our campaign is funding a building, it is not primarily about the building. It's about taking people on a spiritual journey beginning with a faith commitment. Also, it took the pressure off of us as leaders who ask for money. We could entrust the decision to God and the givers; we simply invited them to raise the question with him.

Sometimes people came to the lunch armed with their commitment and eager to share their decision. One of our lead givers, intimately familiar with the project, said he wanted to give 1 percent of the total cost, so that was what his family was committing. Other couples came and heard us out and then came back later with their revised commitment. From those meetings came gifts that far exceeded our expectations, while other gifts fell short and made us feel, quite honestly, as if we had wasted our time. That is probably the nature of any capital campaign. Some people will blow you away with their generosity, and others will disappoint you. It's all part of the ride.

Overall, we did about sixty or so one-on-one lunches (and that's a lot of crab cakes). The lunches had two positive effects: spiritual growth in our lead givers and growing momentum for our campaign. Regarding commitments, we raised a little over 30 percent of what we needed for the total project.

We also had great stories of lives changing. Our friend Bill still talks about how he and his wife, Mary, prayed about their gift after our lunch, just as we had asked them to. This exercise led them to give at a higher level than they had originally planned, and the process actually blessed and strengthened their marriage. Another couple, Neal and Sandy, made a very handsome commitment with the comment: "We want you to know this is the biggest commitment we have ever given to anything, anywhere, ever!" Reading those words was incredibly humbling.

# Going Public

In Lent of 2014, we launched our campaign for the whole church with a message series. We decided to call the series, like the campaign, Vision, since that's what we were inviting people into. We thought that was particularly fitting for this effort. God had given us a vision, and he had appointed the time for making it a reality.

As we counseled in chapter 7, raising givers and moving people to give to their church is ultimately a spiritual exercise, best begun in prayer. A capital campaign most especially needs a prayerful foundation. For our Vision Campaign we began on Ash Wednesday with a forty-hour program of eucharistic adoration. From 6:00 a.m. Wednesday to 10:00 p.m. Thursday, the whole parish was invited to come and pray for the upcoming campaign.

Different staff members took responsibility for each hour, and we offered a lot of different types of prayer and worship experiences. Not every hour was well attended, by any means, though the overall attendance was fabulous. But the important thing is this: that exercise changed the whole tone of the conversation about the upcoming campaign. It was as if prayer melted away criticism and complaint, answered unanswered questions, and won over hearts that were opposed.

**Tom:** The campaign would unfold through a five-week message series. Michael preached at all weekend Masses. In the first week, we showed a video featuring many of the key leaders who had helped us get to this point. They described the process step by step: our growth, the need for more space, extended study of various options, decisions regarding the details of the project, as well as the decision to move forward at this time. Multiple voices communicated the depth of support from the community: this project was definitely not just something the pastor wanted to do.

After the video, we described our vision for the parish and how the new church would be an expression of it. We also talked about the building itself and mapped out its location on our campus. Of course, we answered many of the questions about the campaign that had been asked in our preliminary one-on-one asks. Finally, laying out how the rest of the series would unfold, we announced its culmination in a parish-wide celebration we named Commitment Weekend. In the final week of the series, every parish household would be invited to make a pledge.

As a side note, unlike other campaigns, we did not announce what we had raised from the quiet phase (which we kept *very quiet* by inviting donors' confidentiality). We wanted the parish to undertake a spiritual journey. So instead of promoting what lead givers or anyone else was giving, we shifted the focus to what God was calling each of us to do individually. Also, we didn't want those we were inviting to give in this phase to feel like second-class citizens, whose gifts were somehow less important.

One other thing that was different about this campaign: our goal. We announced the cost of the project but not the financial goal of the campaign; there was no dollar amount attached to it. Instead we preached the goal of 100 percent participation. That goal was merely meant to be motivational, but by the end of the campaign, something like 90 percent of regular parish givers participated in some way.

In the second week of our series, we talked about the importance of making what we came to call a "faith commitment" to the campaign. We connected this to the first reading that weekend, which told the story of the call of Abraham. We described the campaign as an opportunity to grow in faith through our financial commitments. Introducing that giving chart of ours, we challenged everyone to look up as they journeyed, like Abraham, beyond their comfort zones. After Mass that weekend, we handed out campaign brochures along with the commitment card and, of course, the giving chart. The subsequent two weeks were variations on the same theme, inviting every parishioner and parish family to spend time with this material preparing their commitment card in advance of Commitment Weekend.

Each of the five weeks we set up a large tent outside the church, as a kind of "campaign central." Of course, we needed the tent because we had no space for any display in our existing building, and that told a story in itself. The tent was attached to the front of the building so everyone had to walk through it each weekend, making the campaign hard to miss or ignore. Inside the tent, the display changed weekly. The different displays aimed at engaging people and piquing their interest. There were giveaways such as pens, key chains, and bumper stickers, sometimes snacks too. But the renderings of the new building were consistently on display, and staff and parish leaders were always on hand to answer any questions our members might have. (They had plenty, which is actually a positive sign, indicating interest and engagement.) Being available for questions also helped us to be transparent.

One weekend we displayed sheets of drywall, and parishioners were invited to write the names of people they hoped would one day come to the new church because of their sacrifice. The actual drywall would later be used in the construction of the building, and those names would become a permanent part of the new complex, albeit hidden beneath masonry. This proved to be incredibly popular, with people waiting in long lines to include names. Excitement was growing.

Long before the campaign, we had discussed the final weekend in painstaking detail because we wanted to get it exactly right. We knew it had to be special, even unforgettable, but struggled with *how* to do it. How would the people make a commitment? Should they just drop their cards into the basket during the offertory or turn them in at the door on the way out? Neither seemed special enough. Take it home to mail it in or bring it back? Nope, we might never see the card again.

Finally, we landed on a plan. At the end of Mass, we would invite people to get up out of their seats and come to the altar, bringing their commitment cards with them. In other words, we were going to attempt an old-fashioned altar call. Following our closing prayer, several exceptionally talented members of our staff would lead a kind of pep rally. Over a bed of music, urgent and compelling, growing in intensity, they'd challenge people to come forward and bring their commitments to the altar. Eventually the music would drown out the speakers.

Appropriately, the band would play Chris Tomlin's stirring anthem "Lay Me Down" which sings of the deep sacrifice of an open heart and concludes with the admission we are not our own, we belong to God. This piece inadvertently (and automatically after that weekend) would become the theme song of the campaign.

> **Tom:** That was the plan. The problem was, we had never done anything like this before. We had no idea if it would work.

> **Father Michael:** I was pretty sure it wouldn't. It could come across as an exercise in guilt, shaming people into giving. Perhaps, people might resent it. But then again, if it did work, it could be transformative. And since this whole thing was a gamble anyway, why not give it a try? When the altar call started that weekend, I had planned on quickly exiting, so that if nobody came forward, it wouldn't be awkward or embarrassing (for me). However, in that moment, I found myself unable to move. It was so profoundly powerful, eventually overwhelming. Crowds of people came forward, joyfully making their commitments to the campaign. It proved irresistible. It was truly the most exciting moment in the history of the parish.

The Vision Campaign was off to an amazing start.

## Just Enough, but Never More

We waited anxiously that week as the cards were counted and the commitments calculated. Frankly, that wasn't easy; we definitely encountered difficulties. The information people shared on the cards was often ambiguous. In processing them, we would take a conservative approach. We decided that when the exact commitment was unclear, we looked to the lower estimate.

When all was said and done, the commitments from that single weekend equaled the commitments made during the quiet phase. Put together, that put us at about two-thirds of the way toward the total cost of our project. We felt very good about our position. We had raised about 40 percent more than our professional consultants had projected we could raise.

But then, as we moved to the next phase of construction planning, the cost went up. This wasn't entirely surprising, but deeply disappointing nonetheless. As we assessed the situation, we realized we had raised just enough in commitments to keep moving forward. But we would still have to raise more commitments before we could put a shovel in the ground. Anything less in commitments, and the project would have been so far from our goal that we would have probably needed to run another campaign or significantly scale the project back. Anything more, and, quite honestly, it wouldn't have been the faith exercise it was shaping up to be.

This became a pattern for us throughout our campaign. God would provide just enough to encourage us to move forward, just enough to let us know that the project was in accord with his will, but not so much that we felt comfortable. As we shared this with a pastor friend of ours, he commented, "Yes, God never guarantees a wide path; in fact, I remember something about a narrow one."

## Keep Moving Forward

Our diocese very prudently requires parishes to have half the cash in hand, as well as two-thirds in commitments, before construction can begin. The next year was a time of high hopes and hard work to reach that threshold, as our construction documents took shape. To do it, we needed to raise those commitments. We developed a plan to gain support from individuals who had not committed the first time around as well as from people who were new to the parish. At the same time, we believed we needed a seven-figure gift to even eventually reach our goal. There simply wasn't any path to raise all the money we needed without such a transformative contribution.

We put together a list of people who could make it happen. While we worked to set up meetings with all of them, there was only one prospect who held solid potential. Several other parishioners were trusted members of his corporate team, he had been attending our parish for a while, and his kids were in our sacramental programs. We had met with him early on, before the campaign had really taken off. He had indicated then that he would support the project. A few times during that year, however, we had meetings tentatively set with him, only to be later canceled. We strongly believed that if we could only make our pitch in person, he would be very open to our proposal.

> **Tom:** Finally, a firm date was set. A week before the meeting we drove ninety miles up to Philadelphia for a little coaching from Michael's sister-in-law, Vanessa, who is a professional fundraiser. She helped us put together a plan. Michael practiced his pitch over and over again. It was a very compelling case.

We arrived at his office and gave our names to the front desk. Then we waited. And waited. And waited. Our uneasiness began to grow. Finally, a young lady appeared, saying, "I'm sorry; this is not the way we like to do things, but there has been a mistake. He's not here today. We thought you had been contacted." She then awkwardly offered us coffee.

> **Tom:** I told her that we didn't need any coffee. (Michael graciously accepted a cup; he never passes on coffee.) I felt like Rick, in the movie *Casablanca*, when he gets the note on the train from Ilsa Lund that she can't escape Paris with him and that he is to go on alone. It was a punch to the gut.

**Father Michael:** On the other hand, I felt a sense of relief. I had a lingering cold that had slowed me down and certainly would have negatively affected my presentation.

Eventually we did receive support from this individual, but it wasn't the transformative gift we had hoped to receive. We really admire him, and on the merits of all the good work he does in the larger civic community, we very much wanted him to be our angel donor. It was wishful thinking. But, he can still fill that role another day, and we all remain friends.

Meanwhile, other commitments continued to be received in a steady stream, and they were beginning to add up. Nine months into the campaign, we had added another 15 percent to our total commitments. Many people were ahead of their own pledge fulfillment. A significant number of households fulfilled their three-year pledges in that first year alone. All very positive signs.

## One-Year Anniversary

A few months before the one-year anniversary of our campaign, it was suggested that we invite people who had not yet participated to get on board in a parish-wide way. This would also be an opportunity to invite people who had committed to increase their gift, and those who had completed their gifts to keep giving. A second round of campaigning would be a mistake if the first had been weak, and simply impossible if it had failed. But precisely *because* it had been successful, we could ask for more, inviting people to make a larger commitment.

We agreed this was a good idea, but we faced a snag.

At just that time, the archdiocese was undertaking their annual appeal. The year before they had graciously given us a break from the appeal entirely, as we launched our campaign. But now they needed us to participate. The weekend of the appeal would fall just weeks before our second Commitment Weekend. While we wanted to support their appeal, we greatly feared that it would negatively affect our efforts. Their message was a great one, but different from the message of our campaign. Their case for support was compelling but had nothing to do with our case. Combining the campaigns could create confusion. And when people are confused, they don't give.

The archdiocese agreed to let us "guarantee" our goal if we chose to do so. Guaranteeing meant we would make up the difference of any funds that were not raised through their direct mail campaign. It would also mean we would have to use money from our savings and emergency fund to do so.

> **Tom:** When decision time came, we held a meeting of our strategic leadership team. After much discussion and prayer together, Michael took a vote.

> **Father Michael:** I am the pastor and rightly have the final word on decisions (because the Church is not a democracy). But sometimes I choose to put issues to a vote among my senior advisors when I am unsure of a direction to take. That was certainly the case in this situation. It didn't matter anyway, because the vote split 50/50. Half the group thought we should go ahead and dedicate a weekend to the appeal, while others were sure it would adversely affect our efforts to raise money for the building at the one-year anniversary. So, I broke the tie by deciding to guarantee the archdiocesan goal. I'm glad I did. It was yet another gamble that paid off, keeping our campaign focused and our message strong.

We guaranteed our goal and marched forward to our anniversary weekend, or what we came to call Vision II. During that weekend, we talked again about the basics of the project, so as to refresh the memory of members who had been there the year before and to inform people new to the parish. Once again, we connected the dots between the project and our vision to be a church of growing disciples.

Also, at this point, we informed the congregation that we now had a clearer estimate of the true cost of the project and—guess what?—the price had gone up. Anyone who has ever built a house or remodeled their kitchen could understand that cost overruns almost always happen—easy to understand, but still hard to hear. The message had to be delivered in such a way that it didn't sound as though this project was out of control. While we announced that the price had gone up, we didn't announce by how much. *Why not?* Without context, numbers can confuse. We did have people available to answer that question after Mass one-on-one, but very few people actually asked. We attribute that to the trust that had been built up over time.

As a result of our efforts, at the one-year anniversary, the overall commitments to the campaign rose another 20 percent. We raised a little over $1 million in just one weekend. Fourteen percent of people who had committed the previous year increased their giving, which our consultant described as an exceptionally good response.

With Vision II, we took another solid step toward our goal. While nothing would ever again quite have the energy or impact of the kick-off weekend, Vision II was still an unforgettable experience.

## Go or No Go

About two years into our campaign, in the fall of 2015, our architect and engineers were hard at work completing the construction documents. At that point we had set a highly tentative goal to break ground in the spring of 2016. There was still plenty of work to do, but we thought it important to set an exact date, otherwise the project would remain elusive, and people would lose interest.

Remember, we needed half of the money in cash, as well as two-thirds in commitments, before we could put a shovel in the ground. We met the criteria for the pledges, but we were short of the cash. For a spring groundbreaking to happen, the cash had to be raised that winter.

Fortunately, several of our high-capacity parishioners came through for us at exactly this point. And as we were nearing the end of the year, we enjoyed an infusion of cash from people who chose year-end giving for tax purposes. We also received an unexpected but most welcome bump from donors committed to one-time gifts who gave additional gifts in the campaign's second year.

After some concerted effort and fresh focus, it became clear that we would make our *cash goal* (one-half in hand). But none of us were comfortable going forward with the current level of *commitment* (two-thirds in commitments). All along, our aim had been to raise as much as we could and borrow as little as necessary to complete the project. We did not want to create unnecessary financial pressure serving a debt once the building was completed. Another $1.5 million in commitments was needed in order to confidently move forward.

Then, in early January 2016, we received a totally unexpected blessing. One of our major contributors, Mike, indicated he would *double* his commitment, thereby reducing our shortfall to just $1 million. It felt like a game changer. And yet, moving forward was still a risk. Where was the rest of the money coming from?

**Father Michael:** This was a risk I wasn't willing to take, all alone and on my own. I wanted the full support of our staff and lay leadership.

On a cold, dark January evening, we gathered all our parish leaders together and took time to review where we were and bring everyone up to speed. The whole question essentially came down to this: Do we move forward with construction or wait?

The risk in moving forward was that we had no clear plan for covering our significant shortfall. But it was pointed out by one of our advisors, Mitch, that there was also a significant risk in *waiting*. Our construction budget was based on prices guaranteed by the contractor for only a fixed period of time. If we waited, those costs would increase. We could very well find ourselves in a position in which we would be raising money for a project that just kept getting more expensive.

We took a vote, and it was unanimous. Everyone was in favor of moving forward with groundbreaking that spring.

Our groundbreaking ceremony with the archbishop was a great event that we celebrated at each weekend Mass all weekend long, using the occasion to once again create energy and excitement and a sense of inevitability. Each time we did so, new support for the project always came forward, and this time was no exception.

**Tom:** That weekend one parishioner with great capacity approached me to ask where he could find a commitment card to make a gift to the campaign. This was a very generous individual who, with his wife, supports us in many ways but had said at the beginning of the campaign that he would not be contributing to the new church because building projects are not a part of his philanthropy. We never pressed him on it, respecting his decision. But now it looked as if he'd changed his mind. Maybe he'd caught the spirit of the day.

**Father Michael:** Tom did not share this information with me (part of a lifelong pattern). So, I was surprised to come across our friend's commitment card in the mail one evening that week as I was leaving the office. Excitedly, I called Tom with the news, before even opening the envelope. Tom was anxious to find out what was inside. I love to prolong such moments, so I made him suffer. When I did open the envelope, a check fell out for a very handsome six-figure gift. Even as we congratulated each other on this good news, I took a look at the pledge card itself. It turned out the check was only the first payment on a commitment covering the entire amount of our shortfall. The project would be fully funded.

**Tom:** What was awesome about this gift was the *timing*. It reveals so much about how God uses our financial needs to draw us closer to him. Throughout our campaign, he only gave us enough to take us to the next step, but he was there each step of the way.

# The Cornerstone

Once the construction began, the excitement was palpable, and we took full advantage of it to keep motivating our givers to give and bring still others into the giving circle. Each stage of the project was celebrated: pouring the foundation, steel going up, getting the buildings under roof. One especially happy day was the laying of the cornerstone in the winter of 2017, the first episcopal act of our new auxiliary bishop, Adam Parker.

**Father Michael:** Later that same week I was giving a hard-hat tour (something I did every chance I got) to my friend, Wayne. The cornerstone was positioned in a column near the front door, and after it was set in place we covered it with plywood to protect it from damage during construction. Wayne inquired what the plywood was about and I explained.

Wayne asked what the cornerstone said. I responded that it doesn't "say" anything; it's just inscribed with the year of construction: 2017. And then Wayne asked an interesting question: "What's 2017 in the Bible? Is there a chapter and verse numbered 20:17 anywhere in the Bible, and, if so, what does it say?" I had no idea. He said he would look it up, and that was the end of the exchange.

The next morning, an email from Wayne was waiting for me. He wrote, "Take a look at Luke, chapter 20, verse 17." It reads: "The stone which the builders rejected has become the cornerstone."

In September 2017, we opened our new building with absolutely no debt.

Here are fourteen recommendations we endorse when it comes to any kind of capital campaign.

1. Accept that capital campaigns bring uncertainty, and navigating uncertainty always requires leadership.
2. Seek wise counsel, but filter it through what works in *your parish* and in *your approach to giving*.
3. Spend all the time you need thinking through your project so that you can confidently present it to donors.
4. Pay attention to God's timing.
5. Go first; as the leader you must go first when it comes to giving.
6. Practice one-on-one asks with people you know well who will forgive your mistakes and give you honest feedback.
7. Do the groundwork of meeting with donors in a way that fits your personality and your schedule. Make it less painful by making it more sustainable.
8. Develop a template for individual asks to ensure that they are easy and successful.
9. Don't ask for specific dollar amounts. Ask people to decide on their gift in prayer, and then to give outside of their comfort zone.
10. Understand that it's a marathon, not a sprint. Some people will surprise you with their gifts, and others will disappoint you. This is just part of the process. Let the generous gifts energize you, and don't take anyone's decision not to give personally. Also, don't put anybody's name on anything.
11. Present your campaign to the whole parish in a series of messages over a number of weeks, giving people lots of time to get on board. The pastor should preach the entire series.
12. Create a memorable moment for your Commitment Weekend. Make it a special, not-to-be-missed, never-to-be-forgotten kind of weekend.
13. Know that if it requires faith and trust in God to keep moving, God is probably in it.
14. Persevere in prayer. God brings success in his time; honor it.

# CONCLUSION
## *IT'S NOT ABOUT THE MONEY*

It was never about the money.

—Eddie Cicotte, after the fixed 1919 World Series

Our image of God drives so much of our lives. Many people run away from God because they have the wrong image. They think of God as dark and forbidding. Others might not exactly flee in fear, but they stand at a distance, distrustful of a God they understand to be a cosmic cop. Another common misconception is of a heavenly grandfather, genial and of goodwill, yet detached and disengaged. But these days the most prevalent view would be a deistic one: God created the world and promptly proceeded to abandon it. Simply stated, God is wholly irrelevant.

When it comes to funding our parishes, it is vitally important that we hold the right image of God. Raising givers and the funds we need for our ministry and mission requires discipline and dedication, hard work, and plenty of time. It also requires the Lord. If God is only an obscure or ambiguous idea that may or may not be a myth, then we are all alone and on our own in our stewardship efforts.

The truth is that we are not alone in this work. God our Father is with us.

God is real and really engaged in our efforts. He works in people's hearts, moving them in the direction of generosity. The work we undertake through our stewardship efforts is his work. And he encourages us to work with him. God wants to fund his Church but will not do so without us and our very best efforts.

First Chronicles 29 tells us about a campaign initiated by King David. The king wants to establish a Temple to the Lord in Jerusalem, but God tells him he has too much blood on his hands to build a sacred space. Instead, God says that David's son Solomon will be given responsibility for the project. Rather than bristle or brood about this decision, David determines to set his son up for success. He forms a plan to raise the money needed for the Temple, so Solomon can build it when the time comes.

David assembles the heads of the first families and the leaders of the people. He explains to them that as king he has already been amassing the wealth of the nation to fund this very vision. Now, he himself pledges his own massive fortune. Then, inspired by his example, the people respond in kind by bringing vast amounts of silver and gold, iron and bronze, for the construction of God's house.

David successfully leads the people in giving generously to the Temple. In thanksgiving for this wildly successful effort in fundraising, he prays a lengthy prayer in which he makes this unexpected assertion: "But who am I, and who are my people, that we should have the means to contribute so freely? For everything is from you, and what we give is what we have from you" (29:14).

David, the powerful warrior-king, is humbled by the exercise of stewardship. He marvels in wonder at how it is possible that he has the opportunity to raise funds for the Temple. Despite his amazing lifetime of celebrated achievements, he rejoices in the single fact that he has the opportunity to lead God's people in giving.

It's not about the money. When it comes to funding our mission, it's about the opportunity that has been extended to us in our parishes. This work we do, far from a burden or even a responsibility, is an opportunity given to us by a generous God as a wonderful privilege. And in recognizing this opportunity together with David, we might well ask, "Who are we?" Who are we that we can change and transform lives, and in the process make disciples by preaching and teaching stewardship? Who are we and who are our people that we should have the means to contribute so freely?

While cash is crucial to funding our parishes and ministries, we must constantly be on guard not to make it about the money.

- It's not about the money; it's about loving God and serving him in our generation.
- It's not about the money; it's about loving others and helping them fall in love with their Savior.
- It's not about the money; it's about transforming the world little by little through love.

We serve God, who owns it all. Everything belongs to him. One day everyone will know that. Until then, we've got work to do.

Because in the end, it isn't about money; it's about the eternal impact we can and need to make with money.

# APPENDIX A

## *MONEY IN THE NEW TESTAMENT: 77 PASSAGES YOU SHOULD KNOW*

*Matthew 2:11*

The Magi worship Jesus by offering, among other gifts, gold.

*Matthew 6:1–4*

Jesus teaches us to give alms in secret to ensure that our Father will repay us.

*Matthew 6:19–20*

We are advised to store up treasures in heaven because we can't take material wealth with us.

*Matthew 6:21*

Where your treasure is, there your heart will also be.

*Matthew 6:24*

You cannot serve God and money.

*Matthew 6:25–34*

Do not worry about money, for your heavenly Father will take care of your needs.

*Matthew 8:28–34; Mark 5:1–20; Luke 8:28–39*

Jesus drives demons out of a man suffering possession. They take refuge in a herd of swine. The townspeople demand that Jesus leaves, in part because their property, the livestock, has been destroyed in the process of his healing.

*Matthew 17:24–27*

Jesus pays the Temple tax (by having Peter catch a fish with a coin in its mouth).

*Matthew 18:21–35*

In the parable of the unforgiving servant, the protagonist seeks relief from an enormous debt he owes to his master, but he is unwilling to forgive a much smaller debt someone owes him.

*Matthew 19:16–30; Mark 10:17–31; Luke 18:18–30*

Jesus challenges a rich young man to aspire to perfection by giving away his money. He promises a reward to everyone who sacrifices possessions, or anything, for him.

*Matthew 20:1–16*

In the parable of the vineyard workers, day laborers receive equal pay, even though they do not work equal hours.

*Matthew 21:12–17; Mark 11:15–19; John 2:13–25*

Jesus charges the money changers with making the Temple a den of thieves through their commerce.

*Matthew 22:15–22; Mark 12:13–17; Luke 20:20–26*

Jesus teaches us to pay our taxes.

*Matthew 23:23*

In the midst of criticizing the Pharisees, Jesus commends them for tithing.

*Matthew 25:14–30*

In the parable of the talents, the master rewards his servants who invest his money to grow his wealth.

*Matthew 25:31–46*

Jesus teaches that those who use their money and possessions to feed the hungry, clothe the naked, or give drink to the thirsty will be welcomed into eternal life.

*Matthew 26:6–13; Mark 14:3–9; John 12:1–9*
Jesus praises the woman who breaks a costly jar of perfume to anoint him for burial. He goes on to defend her against those who argue that the gift could have provided money for the poor.

*Matthew 26:14–16; Mark 14:10–11*
Judas betrays Jesus for the promise of money.

*Matthew 27:57–61*
Joseph of Arimathea, "a rich man," offers to pay for a tomb for Jesus' burial.

*Matthew 28:11–15*
The Roman soldiers at Jesus' tomb are bribed to perpetuate the lie that the disciples stole the body of Jesus while they were asleep.

*Mark 10:46–52*
Blind Bartimaeus throws aside his begging cloak (in which he collected coins) in order to approach Jesus and receive his sight.

*Mark 12:41–44; Luke 21:1–4*
Jesus watches what people give to the Temple treasury and praises a poor woman for giving wholeheartedly from her poverty.

*Luke 2:22–24*
Joseph and Mary make a sacrificial offering for Jesus' birth, in accordance with the Law.

*Luke 3:7–14*
John the Baptist preaches the need to repent. In response to his message, the crowds ask what they should do. John tells the crowd, including tax collectors and military personnel who were present, to share what extra they have with the poor. The tax collectors should collect no more than what was appointed, and the soldiers should stop extorting money and be satisfied with their wages.

*Luke 6:24*
Jesus warns the rich to be careful, for they have already received their consolation.

*Luke 6:28*
Giving is encouraged. The gifts we give will be given back to us.

*Luke 7:36–50*
Jesus uses the analogy of two people owing money to a creditor, who forgives the debt, as an image of our relationship with God. The debtor with the greater debt will be more grateful.

*Luke 9:23–27*
We learn that it does not profit us to gain the whole world and lose our souls.

*Luke 10:1–4*
Jesus teaches us to pray for our daily needs.

*Luke 10:29–37*
In the parable of the good Samaritan, one man pays for the comfort and care of a victimized stranger.

*Luke 12:13–20*
There are many forms of greed.

*Luke 12:21*
In the parable of the rich fool, Jesus reflects on the foolishness of storing up treasures for oneself but not for God.

*Luke 12:22–34*
Don't worry about money. Seek first the kingdom of God by giving it away instead.

*Luke 15:8–10*
Jesus teaches the parable of the lost coin, in which recovery of misplaced money is compared to God's attitude toward repentant sinners.

*Luke 16:1–13*
In the parable of the dishonest steward, Jesus advises us to use our money in our best long-term interest.

*Luke 16:19–31*
In the parable of the rich man and Lazarus, the wealthy are punished for doing nothing to help the poor.

*Luke 19:1–10*
After meeting Jesus, Zacchaeus gives half his money to the poor and pays back anyone he has defrauded. Jesus applauds these financial measures.

*Luke 19:11–27*
The parable of the ten gold coins tells the story of the master who commends and rewards his servants who invest his money wisely. He punishes the servant who does not.

*Acts 2:44–45, 4:32*
Believers share their possessions and hold everything in common.

*Acts 4:34*
The Church takes care of the financially needy in their midst.

*Acts 4:37*
Barnabas sells property and puts it at the feet of the apostles.

*Acts 5:1–11*
Ananias and Sapphira lie about what they gave to the Church and are punished for it.

*Acts 8:9–25*
An instruction on simony: you can't buy spiritual gifts.

*Acts 10:2*
The Roman centurion Cornelius is praised for generously giving to the poor, and so he is chosen to counsel Peter.

*Acts 11:27–29*
The disciples determine that each should give according to his ability to help the brothers in Judea suffering from a famine.

*Acts 16:12–15*

Paul drives a demon from a slave girl who enjoyed magical powers as a result of her possession. Her exorcism strips her of these powers, resulting in a loss of income for her owners. The incident is relayed to underscore the economic consequences of accepting Christ.

*Acts 19:19–20*

Magicians are converted to Christ. Subsequently they burn their magical arts books, worth a small fortune, as a sign of their conversion.

*Acts 19:23–40*

Demetrius attacks Paul in Ephesus because he is preaching the Gospel. His concern is that Paul's efforts are negatively impacting the Ephesian economy.

*Acts 20:35*

Paul quotes Jesus as saying, "It is more blessed to give than to receive."

*Romans 13:3–7*

Paul tells the Romans to pay their taxes out of respect for governing authority.

*Romans 15:22–29*

Paul tells the Church of Rome that Macedonia and Achaia are making a contribution to the Church in Jerusalem. He commends this offering as particularly appropriate. Since the Gentiles have shared in the Church in Jerusalem's spiritual blessings, they ought to serve the Church in Jerusalem with material blessings.

*1 Corinthians 16:1–4*

The Corinthians are challenged to set aside and save what they can afford to give to the Church in Jerusalem. Each person should predetermine their gift.

*2 Corinthians 8:1–6*

The Macedonians' generosity is praised. They were asked to give and gave beyond their means.

*2 Corinthians 8:7–14*
Paul encourages the Corinthians to excel in generosity as a sign of love and concern for others. He uses the analogy that Jesus became poor so we might be rich.

*2 Corinthians 8:14*
Surplus, Paul agrees, should be used to supply the needs of others.

*2 Corinthians 9:5*
Planned giving is encouraged.

*2 Corinthians 9:7*
Cheerful giving is encouraged.

*2 Corinthians 9:5–15*
Paul makes the analogy of sowing seeds as giving.

*2 Corinthians 11:7–9*
Local churches should be helping other local churches financially.

*Ephesians 5:1–5; Colossians 3:5*
Greed is idolatry.

*Philippians 4:15–19*
Paul thanks the Philippians for their multiple gifts and is eager for them to continue to give because it will "accrue to their account."

*1 Thessalonians 4:12*
The Church in Thessalonica is encouraged to be self-sufficient.

*2 Thessalonians 3:6–15*
Paul acknowledges that he has worked (as a tentmaker) so as not to be a financial burden on the Thessalonians. Anyone who does not work should not eat.

*1 Timothy 3:3*
Paul applies the dictum: anyone who aspires to bishop should not love money.

*1 Timothy 5:8*
Christians have a responsibility to provide for family members.

*1 Timothy 5:18*
Ministers deserve proper compensation.

*1 Timothy 6:6–8*
We brought nothing into the world and can take nothing out, so we should live in contentment when it comes to money.

*1 Timothy 6:9–10*
Paul warns about the trap of desiring riches. The pursuit of money can lead us away from faith.

*1 Timothy 6:17–19*
Use wealth wisely and well. Rely on God and be rich in good deeds, generous, and ready to share.

*Hebrews 7:1–10*
Abraham made his worship offering in the form of a tithe to the priest Melchizedek.

*Hebrews 11:4*
Abel generously offered a sacrificial gift, while Cain begrudgingly brought a compromised one.

*James 2:1–6*
Don't treat the rich in your midst better than you treat the poor.

*James 4:13–17*
Do not presume the future, especially when it comes to money or profits.

*James 5:1–6*
The rich shouldn't put their trust in riches and must not withhold the proper wages to workers.

*2 Peter 2:14–15*
False teachers can be recognized in the payments they receive for wrongdoing.

*1 John 3:16–18*

As a consequence of Jesus' love for us, we should love others, which means helping brothers in need through worldly goods.

*Revelation 3:14–22*

Jesus tells the Church of Laodicea that their riches have made them lukewarm in their relationship with God.

# APPENDIX B
## *GETTING STARTED: 6 PEOPLE WHO CAN HELP*

No matter what role you play in the parish, you can help raise givers to fully fund your ministry.

## 1: If You're the Pastor

- Commit to giving and using your money in a way that aligns with Jesus' teachings.
- Fast and pray for the members of your parish to grow in giving and generosity.
- Commit to preaching on the topic of money as often as it comes up in the Lectionary. Through your preaching, educate your parishioners on Jesus' teachings regarding money.
- Set a date on the calendar for a stewardship weekend, and appoint members of your staff or volunteers to plan it in detail. Make it special, and have some fun.
- Get to know the high-capacity potential givers in your parish. Ask your finance officer to provide a list of your top fifty givers. Set up meetings that work for your schedule where you can get to know them, thank them for their contributions, and let them know what's going on, what's new, and what's next. Seek their advice.

# 2: If You're the Business Manager or Finance Director

- Commit to giving and using your money in a way that aligns with Jesus' teachings.
- Fast and pray for the members of your parish to grow in giving and generosity.
- Set up electronic giving in your parish. If you already have it, work with the pastor to communicate it to the parishioners. Make automatic or electronic giving as easy and accessible as possible, paying special attention to the giving page on your website.
- Make sure you are available to parishioners and responsive to their questions and concerns.
- Take all the steps you need to take to ensure that the parish maintains a balanced budget.

# 3: If You're a Member of the Parish Staff

- Commit to giving and using your money in a way that aligns with Jesus' teachings.
- Fast and pray for the members of your parish to grow in giving and generosity.
- Look for opportunities to encourage and support your pastor, especially when it comes to preaching and teaching on stewardship.
- Go to your pastor and let him know that you want to raise givers and the level of giving in your parish. Offer your help to design and host a stewardship weekend, putting into practice some of the principles of this book.

- Offer any help you can in identifying the high-capacity potential givers in your parish so that you can develop relationships with them.

# 4: If You're a Member of the Parish Pastoral or Financial Council

- Commit to giving and using your money in a way that aligns with Jesus' teachings.
- Fast and pray for the members of your parish to grow in giving and generosity.
- Look for opportunities to encourage and support your pastor, especially when it comes to preaching and teaching on stewardship.
- Challenge the other council members when it comes to their giving. Start a discussion about how the parish could make a greater investment in stewardship efforts.
- Volunteer to assist on a stewardship weekend by making yourself available to fellow parishioners, answering their questions about parish finances, and building credibility for the campaign.

# 5: If You're a High-Capacity Giver

- Commit to giving and using your money in a way that aligns with Jesus' teachings.
- Fast and pray for the members of your parish to grow in giving and generosity.
- Look for opportunities to encourage and support your pastor, especially when it comes to preaching and teaching on stewardship.
- Ask the pastor or church staff to share with you their vision for the parish. Let them know the projects that excite you and that you would invest in if given the opportunity.

- Offer any help you can in identifying other parishioners with above-average capacity to give.

# 6: If You're a Parishioner

- Commit to giving and using your money in a way that aligns with Jesus' teachings.
- Fast and pray for the members of your parish to grow in giving and generosity.
- Look for opportunities to encourage and support your pastor, especially when it comes to preaching and teaching on stewardship.
- Look for opportunities to serve your parish, especially in ways that might save the church money.
- Discipline yourself and your spending to make progress year by year toward your goal of the tithe.

# APPENDIX C
## PREACHING IT: 3 HOMILIES YOU CAN MAKE YOUR OWN

## Homily 1: Stewardship Sunday / In-Pew Commitment

*From Our Message Series "You're Dead, So Now What?"*
*Scripture: Matthew 25:31–46*

This is the fourth and final week of our series "You're Dead, So Now What?" Today we bring this series to a close. It is also our stewardship weekend, which is the only weekend of the year when we ask our members to evaluate their giving and then make a commitment to giving to our parish. So my job is to somehow connect death to giving to this church.

Through this series we have talked about what happens after we die. This is important to discuss because death is a part of life. Despite advances in modern medicine, the death rate in our nation continues to reach exactly 100 percent. Not everyone will retire, not everyone will get married, not everyone will go to college, but every one of us will die. So to ask about what happens after we die is a very practical question and not just one for philosophers or theologians.

On the surface this is a dumb question because most if not all of us have been to a funeral, and so we know what happens after we die. But that's not what most of us mean by that question. We wonder if there is something more. We wonder because our hearts yearn for something more. The simple presence of the yearning for an afterlife, a yearning for something more, *points* to something more because in every other aspect of life, we see that yearnings are fulfilled. We hunger and yearn for food, and there is food to nourish us. We thirst, and there is water to quench our thirst. We yearn for sleep, and there is rest. We yearn for friendship and companionship, and it exists. And on and on, our yearnings seem to point to their fulfillment.

There is a life after death. Death is not the end but a door to something more. The gospel we read today shows that beyond that door, there are eventually one of two eternal destinations that we will reach.

One place is hell or eternal punishment. And we learn in the gospel we read from Matthew that hell is not God's intention for humanity. Jesus tells us that it was a "fire prepared for the devil and his angels." It is a place for those who refuse the mercy of God. God wills that no one go to hell, but some people choose it. Hell is a place for people who refuse every opportunity to love other human beings. Hell is a place for those who refuse to use the blessings of God to invest in others, especially those who are the weakest. In refusing to love others, they refuse to love the Lord. Their refusal to love others shows that they have refused what Jesus has done for them on the Cross.

The second ultimate destination for us is heaven, a place of eternal life, which Jesus tells us in Matthew's gospel has been prepared for us by our heavenly Father. It is a place of absolute joy and fulfillment and reward. It is a place in which we forever receive the blessings and gifts of God. Jesus tells us it was prepared from the foundation of the world, from the very beginning of creation. It is a place for those who are blessed by the Father. Who are the blessed? The blessed are those who recognize that their life is a gift from God and that all they have is grace and blessing and gift.

Their blessedness stems from their positive response to the hungry, the thirsty, the homeless, the poor, the sick, and the imprisoned. In ultimately accepting God's mercy, kindness, and love, we are to extend that same mercy, kindness, and love to others. It is not about earning heaven. You and I could never be good enough to deserve heaven. Heaven is a perfect place, and we are far from perfect. We can get to heaven through the person of Jesus Christ. Doing good is not about earning heaven. We do good because it is a way to thank God for the good he has done for us. We do good because it changes and transforms our character to be the people God wants us to be. We do good because it shapes us into the type of people who would want to be in heaven.

You don't earn heaven by feeding the hungry, giving drink to the thirsty, clothing the naked, or welcoming the stranger. You don't earn heaven by doing good. Doing good helps you to develop a character that wants to be in heaven, that desires heaven.

It is only people who love God and love people who can actually desire heaven. Our actions matter because they are forming our character. Either we are growing in our desire for heaven and union with God and others, or we're growing in selfishness and a desire to be left alone, which is hell.

What we do on this earth matters. This life doesn't matter less because there is an afterlife. What we do matters and has infinite and eternal consequences. An afterlife does not minimize the importance of our actions but maximizes them.

We love the drama of sports and movies and theater because we're suddenly part of a larger story. But right now we are in a story that will one day lead to glory and victory or to loss and defeat. We are in a story that will one day mean we live happily ever after or we won't.

This life matters and the choices we make matter because everyone spends eternity somewhere. All our lives we are either hurting or helping ourselves on the way to heaven. All our lives we are either hurting or helping people on their way to heaven. Jesus tells us in the gospel we read from Matthew that the two are linked. Caring for those around us, concern and love for others, shapes us into people who can enter into eternal life.

This life matters because it shapes where we will spend eternity. The Church is at the forefront of this battle. The Church is in the trenches reminding people that this world is not all there is. The Church is on the frontlines to remind people that we are not on our own, but have been called into a relationship with our heavenly Father. It is the Church that lets people know that they don't earn heaven and don't ever have to give up on heaven because they will never be good enough, but that we have a Savior who has won heaven for them. It is the Church that reminds us that it is in our own best interest to love the people around us. And it all happens right here at the parish.

This is why I believe that the greatest investment you can make is in your parish. The greatest investment you can make is in local churches that are effectively connecting people to their heavenly Father and helping them to live in light of eternity, in light of this larger reality. Investment in schools and education is important. Investing in charitable organizations and outreach is important. You should do that. I hope you do. But those institutions are temporary. The Church is eternal.

The Church will last forever. Ephesians says this, "And he put all things beneath his feet and gave him as head over all things to the church." God put Jesus over all things, as head of all things, for the Church, "which is his body, the fullness of the one who fills all things in every way" (1:22–23). The Church is God's instrument for building Christ's kingdom that will have no end.

As a parish we are making an eternal difference in people's lives. We are making a difference here in North Baltimore and by our ministry to other churches across the country and around the world. People's lives are changing. People's eternal destinies are changing because of the work of this local parish. People's eternal destinies are changing across the country and world because of this parish:

- Because of your investment in this parish, over 550 church staff members from across the United States and Canada attended our Matter Conference last week to be inspired, encouraged, and equipped to make Church matter in their communities.
- Because of your investment in this parish, 450 children in Haiti are able to go to school on a daily basis and enjoy a hot lunch, often their only full meal of the day.

- Because of your investment in this parish, we are able to build a firm foundation of faith for hundreds of children and students in our youth ministry and religious education programs.
- Because of your investment in this parish, we are able to partner with organizations to free people in our own city from poverty and addiction, as well as bring healing to those suffering from HIV and AIDS. Because of your investment, the hungry are being fed and the homeless given a fresh start.
- Because of your investment in this parish, over 3,500 people come together weekly here at this church or join us online to worship and develop a living relationship with the loving Lord.
- Because of your investment in this parish, you are making it possible for
  - marriages to be revived,
  - families to be put back together,
  - students and young adults to live their life with purpose, and
  - people who are preparing for the next life to live with hope.

Here are some of the lives that are changing because of what we are doing together as a church:

> You know what I find amazing? . . . How you can take messages from the Bible and translate them into life today. . . . It is why we came to Nativity; it is why we love Nativity. Thanks for changing lives!
>
> —Amy

> I feel like our parish has been reborn because of Nativity. Your book has given me the strength to do what I knew needed to be done a decade ago. I've also convinced our entire staff to attend your upcoming Matter Conference. Thank you for being such an inspiration.
>
> —Sue

I love my church. I think great relationships are created and they grow at the right times. Wow, do I love Nativity, you guys, the band, the kids, etc.

—John

On Sunday night when I asked my girls what the best part of their weekend was, both said, "Church!"

—Michelle

So today we ask you to evaluate your financial investment in this parish and its mission. If you have already prayed over your commitment for the coming year, then we invite you to take some time to fill out your card right now. If you need to, take your commitment card home, pray over your commitment this week, and bring the card back next weekend.

Your investment in this church echoes in eternity. It makes an eternal difference.

# Homily 2: Preaching on Money and Greed from the Lectionary

*From Our Message Series "Response Ability"*
*Scripture: Luke 19:1–10*

Welcome to the fourth week of our fall series. To bring you up to speed if you've missed the past weeks of this series, we started off saying that as human beings we have freedom to act and react to life. We have the ability to respond to the events that happen to us. And how we choose to respond determines in large part the course and quality of our life.

When you look back over the arc of your life to date, how you responded to certain situations, certain opportunities, and certain events has shaped the outcomes. Maybe there was a crisis in your life, and instead of rushing off and doing something rash, you slowed down and made a measured response. You can look to that moment as key in your life.

Or some opportunity was given, and maybe you took full advantage of it and ran that opportunity all the way down the field, and that changed everything.

Or you didn't—and you regret it.

What is true in life is also true in our faith life. God, who created the universe and is the origin of absolutely everything, always takes the initiative in granting his grace and mercy. His gifts are given to us each and every day, and it is up to us to take responsibility to acknowledge that.

When good things happen to us, there is a moment, a decision point, in which we decide to turn back to God or not. We can choose to ignore the gift we've been given or the fact that it even was a gift. We just keep on going, as if nothing is different than before.

When we do respond, well, that's called prayer. So we have looked at responding to God through prayer. We talked about prayer of thanksgiving. God gives to us, we acknowledge with gratitude. We've also looked at how we respond to God when it feels as if we are *failing in prayer* or it seems God is not even listening to us or ignoring us. And we said in those times it is our responsibility to *keep on praying* and keep on praying and keep on praying.

God may seem silent, prayer may not seem to be making any difference, we may feel like prayer failures, but that is precisely when we need to persevere in prayer, stay in the conversation. By extending the conversation, you develop the relationship God wants with you. Maybe you've heard people talk about having a personal relationship with Christ, and you've thought, "I don't even know what that means." Well, initially it's just a conversation.

Last week we looked at how to be more effective at prayer. And we learned that our prayer is not based on our performance but on our heart. Effective prayer, prayer that puts us in a right relationship with God and connects us to him, is made with a humble heart. We humble ourselves when we admit we need God's mercy, admitting our need to atone for our sins.

This week, we are going to shift gears a bit and for the next three weeks, we will talk about our response and ability when it comes to our money and financial life.

Believe it or not, money is a spiritual issue. To begin with, the money and possessions placed in your hands don't really belong to you. They belong to God. You are God's money manager. You may push back and say, "I've earned my money. I worked hard for it." And I am sure that's true. But even your ability to do that is God's gift. Ultimately it all comes from him. And more than that, it's all going back to him.

Here's proof that your money and possessions really don't belong to you. There was a time when you didn't have what you now have in your possession, and there will be a time when you no longer have it. Eventually the money you have is going to someone else. You don't really own it. You are God's money manager, whether you accept that title or not. How you use the money that God has placed in your hands and given you *greatly affects* your character and your relationship with God.

Either you will use money and possessions to grow in love for God and love for others, or your money and possessions will corrupt your heart and soul. How you respond to the money God has given you greatly affects your relationship with God and others and your spiritual health.

We are going to look today at the story of a man who perfectly illustrates this point. We are in a book of the Bible called Luke, where in chapter 19 we read that Jesus "came to Jericho and intended to pass through the town" (Lk 19:1). Jesus is on a road trip to Jerusalem. This is toward the end of his life when he is going to Jerusalem to die on the Cross. Jericho is about twenty miles from Jerusalem so not very far from his final destination.

"Now a man there named Zacchaeus . . . was a chief tax collector and also a wealthy man" (Lk 19:2). If you were here last week, you remember that we described tax collectors as the most despised people in the community. They were Jews who worked for the Romans to collect taxes from other Jews in order to pay for the Roman occupation of Israel. Not only that, but the Romans didn't care how much tax collectors collected as long as they got their share. So often tax collectors took exorbitant amounts of money from their fellow countrymen, far above what the Romans required, and pocketed the difference. They could essentially steal from their fellow countrymen because they had the power of the Roman army behind them. And apparently Zacchaeus had taken full advantage of his position, because he wasn't just a tax collector but the chief one.

Luke goes on to tell us that "Zacchaeus was seeking to see who Jesus was; but he could not see him because of the crowd, for he was short in stature. So he ran ahead and climbed a sycamore tree in order to see Jesus, who was about to pass that way" (Lk 19:3–4).

So this guy is out there on the edge of the crowd. He didn't have any place in the circle of the community. Sort of like Scrooge at Christmas, everybody was having a great time but him. It's evident that Zacchaeus pursued money to the point of greed—that is to say, mastery over his life (it is scarcely likely he could have achieved his corrupt position without money). In turn, his greed left him all alone. Ultimately, that's what greed does.

The approach of Jesus for some reason awakens something inside of the guy. He runs out ahead of the crowd, not the usual comportment of a high-ranking official. And then he does something really unexpected for someone of his rank and position: he climbs a tree. It is a spiritual exercise, because he is seeking Christ in the process. It is also symbolic because this man, up until this point, has been completely absorbed in earthly, mundane pursuits, and here he is, in a sense, reaching up to higher pursuits.

Luke continues, "When he reached the place, Jesus looked up and said to him, 'Zacchaeus, come down quickly, for today I must stay at your house.' And he came down quickly and received him with joy" (Lk 19:5–6). Zacchaeus just wants a glimpse of Jesus, but as is usual with Jesus, he gives more than expected or imagined. Instead of Zacchaeus just getting a glimpse of Jesus, Jesus asks to come stay at his house. Luke says that Zacchaeus responds to this invitation by coming down from the tree quickly. In other words, he doesn't pause; he doesn't think about it. The invitation to hang out with Jesus is so enticing that he simply goes for it.

This was the personality of Jesus. People who were nothing like him *liked him*; they were drawn to him and wanted to be with him. And if you think about it, if that's the way Jesus was, shouldn't that be the way his Church is? As a church community, we should reflect the attractiveness of Jesus, so that people who are far from God feel comfortable about getting a little closer to him.

Luke goes on to say that when the crowd "saw this, they began to grumble, saying, 'He has gone to stay at the house of a sinner'" (Lk 19:7). This shows us how much of a loner Zacchaeus had become and how much the crowd following Jesus, for all their enthusiasm, didn't get it.

Anyway, Jesus and Zacchaeus spend some time together. How much time? Don't know. What did they discuss? Doesn't say. Luke only tells us they dined together and enjoyed a conversation. As a result of the conversation, Luke tells us: "Zacchaeus stood there and said to the Lord, "Behold half of my possessions, Lord, I shall give to the poor, and if I have extorted anything from anyone I shall repay it four times over" (Lk 19:8). Jesus responds, "Today salvation has come to this house, because this man too is a descendant of Abraham. For the Son of Man has come to seek and to save what was lost" (Lk 19:9).

The *conversation* leads to *conversion*. Zacchaeus has a total change of heart and forms a plan for a total change of life. This is such an amazing response that we could do a whole series on it. Salvation is God's saving action. Elsewhere the Bible says: "God our savior . . . wills everyone to be saved and to come to knowledge of the truth" (1 Tm 2:3–4). Salvation means that God had rescued Zacchaeus from the prison and isolation of greed and gave him a new lease on life. That's what God does in our lives.

Now I am going to offend you, but there is a little of the old Zacchaeus in each of us. And as with Zacchaeus there is an opportunity for something better. Zacchaeus's sin was greed. He loved money to the point that he allowed it to master him and destroy his relationships. Probably nobody is exactly like that here. But you struggle with it from time to time, and so do I. We can't live in our consumer culture and not feel the pull and tug of greed. It's impossible. And what makes this particular problem an especially difficult one is that it is so hard for us to see greed in the mirror.

One night this week I ran out for carryout. The check was twenty dollars. I realized I only had twenty-five dollars (I thought I had a lot more). Anyway, I paid and then left, and on the way out there was a man there who asked me for money. I lived in Baltimore City for a while, and I have encountered a lot of con artists who do this for a living. But for some reason this guy's appeal touched my heart, I had immediate empathy for him, and I wanted to give him money. Lots of times when you feel that way, it is God who is calling you to do it. That was my first thought. My second was this: I only have five dollars, and I thought I had a lot more. And that thought closed my heart. I averted my eyes and got into my car.

I'm happy to say I had a third thought and got out of the car and handed him the five dollars. And I am not telling this story to try to look good, but only to suggest that the struggle is real for everyone. And for some of you, if you could come to identify greed and recognize it in yourself, there would be a huge breakthrough in your relationship with God and in your relationship with others.

Some of you struggle with greed when it comes to your possessions. No one wants to borrow anything from you because they don't want to have to put up with the anxiety of having to bring it back exactly perfect, and they know you'll notice.

For some of you, friends and family don't want to go to your house because they can't feel comfortable there. You are so worried about your stuff and what might happen to your stuff when they are there. Your family members feel as though your possessions have a place in your heart above them.

For some of you, you simply need to start giving to the poor like Zacchaeus did. God has called you to release some of your money to help the hungry or the homeless or to drill wells for water or help mothers in crisis pregnancies or helping to save and transform our city—and you haven't released that money, even though God is calling you to do so.

You may be like Zacchaeus because you *owe someone* money. Maybe you have taken some money. You have cheated someone, you have stolen from someone and you owe them money. Maybe they don't even know you have stolen from them. You could be a teenager and you take from your parents all the time and they just don't notice. Maybe you are so smart with money, people don't know you have taken it, but you know you owe them.

Or is there a bill you haven't paid? You received the service either personally or for your business, but you just don't feel like paying it. And maybe it is a business deal and you know the system well enough: The alternative for them is to sue you and you know it just isn't worth it for them. But in your heart, you know you should pay the bill and that would be the God-honoring thing to do. Or maybe there are some personal bills you should pay, and you keep putting them off.

Maybe your form of greed comes in cheating your employer—you're not really working to earn the money you make. Are you only putting in half the effort and getting away with it? Or do you need to recognize that you are being greedy when all you ever do with your money is spend it on yourself.

And let me tell you, the more defensive you feel right now, the greater possibility that greed is a problem for you. Recognize this as a spiritual issue and pray about it. Have a conversation with God, and in that conversation look for where you need conversion.

Give back what you've taken. Make restitution on what you've stolen. Pay your bills . . . pay back what you owe. Stop spending all your money on yourself. Give your stuff away instead.

Make all of that a part of your response to God's blessings.

# Homily 3: Mission Appeal Sunday

*From Our Message Series "Your Best Yes"*
*Luke 3:3–14*

Welcome to the third week of a series we are calling "Your Best Yes." It hardly needs saying—it's a complete cliché to say it at all—but you are probably already in the thick weeds of the most hectic time of the whole year, a time that will fly by in no time at all, while sometimes feeling as though it will never come to an end.

Whether you like it or not, we're all in the same boat with limited time and resources, facing everything that will be coming our way over the next month. And as we said last week, here's the problem: it's all good. It's all good, but it doesn't always all fit into our schedules, especially since the rest of life proceeds more or less as usual. We've still got to do everything and deal with everything we're currently dealing with that does not go on hold or go away just because the holidays are here.

That's part of the problem. The other part of the problem is that it can be difficult to know what to do, and then what to do next, and, of course, what not to do at all. It is a good problem. It means we are blessed in many ways with many things.

But it is a problem nonetheless. All the good stuff can start to feel like pressure. Maybe there is no avoiding the busyness. But we don't have to be anxious, angry, or annoyed. There is a big difference between being busy and being anxious, angry, and annoyed because we're busy.

And if you step back and think about it, the holiday season is like a microcosm of the whole of life. Because the whole of life is an ever-changing menu of options and choices and decisions that just keep coming our way. And regardless of whether we are deliberate or thoughtful about it, what we're doing with those options and choices and decisions is determining the quality and direction of our lives.

What we need is a strategy. We need a plan—for the holidays for sure, but really moving forward into the New Year—for more sustainable, successful living. Last week, we laid out one such strategy. It's called *discernment.*

Discernment is about judgment, but not just decision-making. It's much more about sensitivity and even shrewdness when it comes to decision-making. Discerning is not just separating the good from the bad, but the good from the greater good, and the greater good from the great-est good. When life presents more than one good option, discernment is about reflecting on the best one, the one that represents the best use of our time and resources, the one that will have the greatest impact or do the most good—the greatest good before God.

God actually wants to get involved and really can help us out when it comes to making good and great decisions in life and about life.

- God wants us to make positive, healthy, life-giving choices.
- God wants to lead us down the path of abundant life.
- God wants us to see every day of our lives as a gift and not just some-thing we need to get through.

So many people approach the Christmas season as something to get through. That's not how God wants us to live. We will find the best yes when we invite God into our decision-making process.

Discernment is also about understanding we do have a choice. We always have a choice. God made you free to make decisions, and you have the capacity to choose. He made you capable of discernment. So often we act as if we have no choice when it comes to what we have to do, especially at Christmas. When we only act or make decisions out of an obligation and a sense of duty, there's every chance we're working against our own personality types—working against who God made us to be—in ways that are probably self-defeating, in ways that are acting against God's will or what God desires for us.

You choose to say yes, just like you can choose to say no. And the best way to know when to say yes and when to say no is to base your discern-ment in love. That's really what this series is all about, discernment in love.

Over the course of this series we're looking at how we can grow to love God, love others, and, inspired by that love, make disciples through our very best yes. Last week we talked about loving God by trusting him. To really love God is to trust God.

Today we want to look at a simple way we can grow in our love for people over the holidays. To help us we are going to look at a passage from Luke's gospel, which we began to look at last Sunday. These readings are the traditional ones for Advent. Luke introduces us to John the Baptist. John was a cousin of Jesus who had been chosen by God to be a preacher and prophet. He is usually considered the last and greatest of all the prophets in the Bible. His message, as we saw last week: "Prepare the way of the Lord, make straight his paths. Every valley shall be filled and every mountain and hill shall be made low. The winding roads shall be made straight, and the rough roads made smooth, and all flesh shall see the salvation of God" (3:4–6).

Whenever a king or some powerful and important person was expected somewhere, workmen would go before him to do roadwork. They would smooth out the rough patches and make the crooked paths straight, generally creating a clearer, easier path so that the king's arrival would be faster and more efficient. The king whom John is anticipating is Jesus. John recognizes Jesus as the King of kings, the Son of God, the long-awaited Savior who was to come into the world.

The illustration of the roadwork is a metaphor for a kind of spiritual preparation. John himself called this "repentance." The word *repent* is all about three things really: a change in thinking, which leads to a change of heart, which eventually leads to a change in behavior.

John was rather like a rock star. Huge crowds of people were attracted to hear him speak, and when they did, they were moved to repentance and, subsequently, baptism. Their change in thinking and change of heart lead them to reexamine their behavior. So, they ask, obviously enough, "What then should we do?" (Lk 3:10).

John's answer probably disarmed many of his listeners for its simplicity. He says, "Whoever has two tunics should share with the person who has none. And whoever has food should do likewise" (Lk 3:11). If you have extra, if you have more than you need, share with those who have less than you. Share with those who don't have anything at all. Sharing is a basic component of nature and creation. In fact, the whole process of creation, the way in which it was made to work, relies on the concept of sharing. It is how God formed creation to grow and go; from flowers and fruit to bees and babies, they are all the product of sharing.

John's profound prophetic instruction is basically the same encouragement I would give to my four-year-old niece: share. Simply share what you have. That's how it was meant to be, but as with many things sin obscures and confuses this process. We misunderstand the idea, or we simply forget—besides the fact that sometimes we just don't want to do it.

This was my experience this past week. There was a young man in front of Starbucks selling cookies for a charity that helps out other kids in Baltimore City Schools, as he explained when I passed by. I was impressed that such a young fellow would be willing to stand out in the cold and so articulately make his pitch to those who passed by, most of whom completely ignored him. I didn't want the cookies, but I thought I would help him out, if nothing else than to encourage him. I opened my wallet and I had a five and a ten. I actually started to reach for the ten and impulsively gave him the five instead. Of course, I spent more than that inside Starbucks.

Often times we just stifle the thought of sharing and giving; it's so ingrained in us to hold on to stuff instead. That's why it's really a spiritual issue that is part of the process of repentance John talked about: changing our thinking, to change our feeling, to change our behavior. A basic way in which we love one another is by sharing.

The Christmas season is above all the season of sharing. And sometimes it is most compelling when it's done for people we don't even know, people who may never repay us or even thank us. Every year at Christmas we try as a parish to undertake a giving and service project on behalf of one of our mission partners, and this year we have a simply extraordinary opportunity.

We are going to build a high school. Really, we're really going to build a high school for the Anawin Home Orphanage in Abuja, Nigeria. Nativity has an established history with the orphanage reaching back to

2007, and a strong and mutually respectful association with our mission partners there, the Missionary Sisters of the Poorest of the Poor.

The sisters rescue and raise some of the most vulnerable children in their country. Due to some very unfortunate superstitions in the culture there, people sometimes literally discard babies—just leave them by the side of the road or throw them away in the trash. The sisters rescue and raise these children, giving them home, health, and hope.

For several years in Advent, Nativity has sponsored projects that have dramatically enhanced the quality of life at the orphanage. A critical part of taking responsibility for the love, care, and growth of these children means removing all barriers to a quality education. Right now, they have an elementary school at the orphanage, but after graduating the children have no next step.

We want to change that; this Christmas we want to build a high school. A high school will change and transform the lives and the futures of those boys and girls. And the great thing about building the school is that it will be entirely sustainable. In addition to the orphans, the school will be open to children from the town whose parents can afford tuition. So, the school will be self-funding once constructed.

After Mass you can go out to the tent on the plaza and "buy a brick" to make the school happen. In exchange we'll give you a small decorative ornament that you can give as a gift to someone on your Christmas list. Instead of another sweater or gift card, give the gift of education and hope.

The total cost of the school is $80,000, which we've no doubt this parish can raise in one day. We want to surprise the sisters with the whole amount as our Christmas gift.

Probably most of us are familiar with John the Baptist and his role in the Christmas story. Every year we are used to hearing his announcement to prepare and to share. But we shouldn't allow the familiarity of the message to mask the impact of the message. John's announcement concerns the advent of grace and truth that is the coming of Christ. And that coming changes everything. At least it can.

This Christmas forget the anxiety, anger, anxiousness. Invite the grace and truth of Christ into your busyness.

Choose to give God your best yes.

*Videos of these complete message series and many others are available through the Rebuilt Parish Association: rebuiltparishassociation.com.*

# APPENDIX D
## *STEWARDSHIP SUNDAY:*
## *5 TIPS YOU CAN USE*

Once a year, and only once a year, we take a weekend to reflect on financial commitment to our local parish church. The following are five practices we've found helpful in hosting a successful stewardship weekend, one that receives a positive response and solid commitments for giving.

## Tip 1: Exercise Discipline throughout the Year

Our Stewardship Sunday is a success because of the discipline we impose on ourselves throughout the rest of the year. We host no fundraisers, ever, we have no second or special collections, and we never sell anything in our lobby. Of course, we talk about money as often as it comes up in the Lectionary (which is often), but we only talk about giving to our parish once a year. This discipline ensures that the congregation is open to the message when we preach it.

# Tip 2: Prepare the Congregation on the Preceding Weekend

So that no one is surprised or blindsided, we give plenty of advanced notice that Stewardship Sunday is coming, although because it's on the same weekend every year, most people are expecting it. They also know it's probably not the optimum weekend to invite guests. We choose the weekend before Thanksgiving, because we think of our offering as an act of thanksgiving. In this way, our "ask" comes at the beginning of the holiday season and the end of the calendar year, which is a time of generosity and giving in our culture. We actually distribute commitment cards in the weeks prior to the stewardship weekend to encourage people to take time to think about and pray about their gift. Obviously, this, in turn, yields more thoughtful, prayerful commitments.

## Tip 3: Carefully Craft the Message

Our message on Stewardship Sunday is carefully crafted to focus on thanksgiving as a worship offering. We talk about *giving in your place of worship as an act of worship.*

## Tip 4: Preach the Four *P*s

We rely on four basic principles for giving, the ladder of giving we spoke of in chapter 7, which we repeat religiously each year. We want parishioners to give in a way that is *planned* and a *priority* in their budget. We also challenge people to give a *percentage* of their income, whatever the percentage, but always keeping in mind the biblical standard of the tithe, or 10 percent. And we further challenge everyone to commit to *progress* in their percentage each year, moving closer to the tithe, and eventually beyond it.

# Tip 5: Make It a Celebration

While many pastors and parishioners alike dread this annual exercise, we try to turn it into a celebration. We always include humor in the homily, to get people smiling, because when they smile and laugh, they relax. And when they relax, they're usually more open to our message. Toward that end, we usually also add some fun element, like a video making fun of ourselves. We like to have some snack or treat to give away after Mass to encourage fellowship.

On Stewardship Sunday we always host our annual parish business meeting. It is open to everyone and run by our parish financial officers and financial council. They present the previous year's budget and answer questions about income and expenses. That this meeting is usually not very well attended, we believe, is a positive sign that people are generally satisfied with how we're handling their money. But it is important that everyone know we offer this meeting for purposes of transparency and accountability.

# APPENDIX E
## *HOW WE DO IT: 3 VIDEO RESOURCES YOU CAN WATCH*

Throughout the book, video resources we have used in our parish to encourage and promote giving have been referenced. Basically, they fall into three categories and can be found at https://rebuilt-parish.com/churchmoney.

## Video Resource 1: Giving Moments

Over the last few years we have developed brief video announcements we've come to call "giving moments." They are one- to two-minute videos that describe the various ministries in our parish. These videos remind our parish members what their giving funds and the impact it has. They underscore the importance and value of giving to the parish. Just as companies advertise to their existing customers to reinforce the value of their products, it is important that we remind our parishioners why their giving matters.

## Video Resource 2: Capital Campaign

Engaging in a capital campaign can be one of the most intimidating and frightening experiences for parish leaders. We can help. We produced a series of videos to introduce and launch our capital campaign. In one video, parish leaders explain the critical path and all the behind-the-scenes planning that led us to undertake a campaign. Another video illustrates how we invited members to make their commitment. There is also one that offers a look at our campaign's Commitment Weekend.

## Video Resource 3: Message Series

These are homilies used at Church of the Nativity in past years regarding stewardship, mission appeals, and special appeals. Included here are homilies about money and giving as the theme comes up in the Lectionary. Homily transcripts are also available.

# REFERENCES AND RESOURCES

Alcorn, Randy. *The Treasure Principle*. Colorado Springs, CO: Multnomah, 2005.

Carter, Doug M. *Raising More than Money: Redefining Generosity Reflecting God's Heart*. Nashville, TN: Thomas Nelson, 2007.

Cloud, Henry. *9 Things You Simply Must Do: To Succeed in Love and Life*. Nashville, TN: Thomas Nelson, 2004.

Council of Trent. "Tithes Are to Be Paid in Full: Those Who Withhold Them Are to Be Excommunicated. The Rectors of Poor Churches Are to Be Piously Supported," session 25, chap 12.

Cruze, Rachel, and Dave Ramsey. *Smart Money, Smart Kids*. Brentwood, TN: Lampo, 2014.

González, Justo L. *Faith and Wealth: A History of Early Christian Ideas on the Origin, Significance, and Use of Money*. Eugene, OR: Wipf and Stock, 1990.

Hanna, Frank. *What Your Money Means and How to Use It Well*. New York: Crossroad Publishing, 2008.

Heath, Chip, and Dan Heath. *Switch: How to Change When Change Is Hard*. New York: Broadway Books, 2010.

Keller, Timothy. *Counterfeit Gods: The Empty Promises of Money, Sex, and Power, and the Only Hope that Matters*. New York: Penguin Group, 2009.

Kreeft, Peter. *Back to Virtue*. San Francisco: Ignatius Press, 1992.

Lewis, C. S. *Mere Christianity*. San Francisco: HarperOne, 2015.

*Michael Hyatt Podcast.* "Banish the Guilt of Making Money: 4 Reasons You Should Never Feel Conflicted." https://michaelhyatt.com/season-5-episode-09-banish-the-guilt-about-making-money-podcast.

Nouwen, Henri. *The Spirituality of Fundraising.* Nashville, TN: Upper Room Books, 2010.

Ortberg, John. *When the Game Is Over It All Goes Back in the Box.* Grand Rapids: Zondervan, 2007.

Ramsey, Dave. *The Total Money Makeover.* Nashville: Thomas Nelson, 2003.

Rosner, Brian. *Greed as Idolatry: The Origin and Meaning of a Pauline Metaphor.* Grand Rapids: William B. Erdmans Publishing Company, 2007.

Senge, Peter M. *The Fifth Discipline: The Art and Practice of a Learning Organization.* New York: Doubleday, 1990.

Sinek, Simon. *Start with Why.* New York: Portfolio/Penguin, 2011.

Stanley, Andy. *Fields of Gold.* Carol Stream, IL: Tyndale House, 2004.

United States Conference of Catholic Bishops. *Stewardship: A Disciple's Response.* Washington, DC: USCCB, 2009.

Warren, Rick. *Purpose Driven Life.* Grand Rapids, MI: Zondervan, 2002.

Willard, Dallas. *The Divine Conspiracy: Rediscovering Our Hidden Life in God.* New York: HarperCollins, 1997.

———. *The Spirit of the Disciplines: Understanding How God Changes Lives.* New York: HarperCollins, 1988.

Yancey, Philip. *Money: Confronting the Power of a Modern Idol.* Portland, OR: Multnomah, 1985.

Zech, Charles. *Why Catholics Don't Give.* Huntington, IN: Our Sunday Visitor, 2006.

# REBUILT RESOURCES

Church of the Nativity in Timonium, MD. ChurchNativity.com. On Facebook at facebook.com/churchnativity. On Twitter @nativitypastor.

"LIVE!" Nativity's Online Campus. live.churchnativity.com.

Rebuilt Parish. RebuiltParish.com.

RebulitParish.com/churchmoney.

Rebuilt Parish Association. RebuiltParishAssociation.com.

Rebuilt Parish Conference (Nativity's Annual Parish Conference). RebuiltConference.com.

*Rebuilt* Podcast. https://rebuiltparish.podbean.com.

White, Michael. *Make Church Matter* (blog). NativityPastor.tv.

White, Michael, and Tom Corcoran. *Rebuilding Your Message: Practical Tools to Strengthen Your Preaching and Teaching.* Notre Dame, IN: Ave Maria Press, 2015.

———. *Rebuilt: Awakening the Faithful, Reaching the Lost, Making Church Matter.* Notre Dame, IN: Ave Maria Press, 2013.

———. *Rebuilt: The Field Guide.* Notre Dame, IN: Ave Maria Press, 2016.

———. *Tools for Rebuilding: 75 Really, Really Practical Ways to Make Your Parish Better.* Notre Dame, IN: Ave Maria Press, 2013.

**Rev. Michael White** is a priest of the Archdiocese of Baltimore and pastor of Church of the Nativity in Timonium, Maryland. He earned his bachelor's degree from Loyola University Maryland and his graduate degrees in sacred theology and ecclesiology from the Pontifical Gregorian University in Rome.

During White's tenure as pastor at Church of the Nativity, the church has almost tripled in weekend attendance. More importantly, commitment to the mission of the church has grown, evidenced by the significant increase of giving and service in ministry, and much evidence of genuine spiritual renewal. White is the coauthor of *Rebuilt*—which narrates the story of Nativity's rebirth—*Tools for Rebuilding, Rebuilding Your Message*, and *The Rebuilt Field Guide*.

**Tom Corcoran** has served Church of the Nativity in Timonium, Maryland, in a variety of roles that give him a unique perspective on parish ministry and leadership. First hired as a youth minister, Corcoran has also served as coordinator of children's ministry and director of small groups. He is lay associate to the pastor and is responsible for weekend message development, strategic planning, and staff development.

Corcoran is the coauthor of *Rebuilt*—which narrates the story of Nativity's rebirth—*Tools for Rebuilding, Rebuilding Your Message*, and *The Rebuilt Field Guide*.

churchnativity.com
rebuiltparish.com
rebuiltparish.podbean.com
Facebook: churchnativity
Twitter: @churchnativity
Instagram: @churchnativity

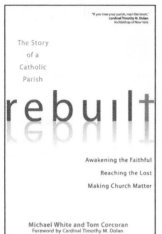